EUROPEAN
DREAM HOMES

SECOND EDITION

200 French, English and Mediterranean Designs

⬡ HOME PLANNERS®

European Dream Homes, 2nd Edition

Published by Home Planners, LLC
Wholly owned by Hanley-Wood, LLC
Editorial and Corporate Offices:
3275 West Ina Road, Suite 110
Tucson, Arizona 85741

Distribution Center:
29333 Lorie Lane
Wixom, Michigan 48393

Jayne Fenton, President
Jennifer Pearce, Vice President, Group Content
Linda B. Bellamy, Executive Editor
Arlen Feldwick-Jones, Editorial Director
Vicki Frank, Managing Editor
Sarah P. Smith, Project Editor
Laura Hurst Brown, Project Editor
Matthew S. Kauffman, Graphic Designer
Sara Lisa, Senior Production Manager
Brenda McClary, Production Manager

Book Design by Matthew S. Kauffman

Front Cover:
Design HPT880011 ©Stephen Fuller, Inc.
Photo courtesy of Stephen Fuller, Inc.
To view floor plans, see page 24.

Back Cover:
Design HPT880004 ©Archival Designs, Inc.
Photo by Ron Kerr, Kerr Studios
To view floor plans, see page 12.

Title Page:
Design HPT880200 ©Living Concepts Home Planning
Photo by Carolina Photo
To view floor plans, see page 16.

Facing Page:
Design HPT880201 ©Stephen Fuller, Inc.
Photo by Dave Dawson
To view floor plans, see page 17.

©2002 Home Planners, LLC

10 9 8 7 6 5 4 3 2 1

Printed in the United States of America

Library of Congress Control Number: 2002102739
ISBN softcover: 1-931131-05-8

CONTENTS

Photo courtesy of David Marc Loftus, Archival Designs, Inc.

An Introduction to European Architecture

Photo by Bob Greenspan ©Alan Mascord Design Associates, Inc.

From whimsical cottages to stately manors, European homes have a distinctive flair, offering wonderful detailing and an Old World look. In general, French and English homes feature exteriors of stone, brick and stucco, alone or in combination. Decorative stickwork is common, as are small-pane windows and keystone arches, often with double rows of bricks or stones. Roofs may be either hip or gabled, with a variety of interesting planes and angles and a wide use of dormers. Except for styles such as Tudor or Norman, there are few definitive differences between French and English homes.

Employing many of these characteristics, a popular design, particularly for larger houses, is the French or English country home: a long, low-slung structure, frequently using a breezeway to connect house and garage. Manor houses are also large yet more symmetrical—even square in shape—resulting in a stately, more massive appearance. At the opposite end of the spectrum is the cottage, irregular in shape and described by such adjectives as whimsical, eccentric and quaint. In fairy tales, cottages are small, but in a book of dream homes you will find they come in all sizes.

Half-timbering is a feature usually associated with English styles, but it can also be a decorative accent on French farmhouses. Typically one- or 1½-stories

4

Photo courtesy of Stephen Fuller, Inc.

OPPOSITE ABOVE: A stone-and-stucco facade defines this highly livable French chateau; page 21. LEFT: Wrought-iron details and gently flared eaves enrich this French Country exterior; page 25. BELOW: Articulated details and symmetry characterize Neoclassical style, derived from the Mediterranean revival vernacular; see page 12. BELOW LEFT: Uncoursed stonework and half-round arches exhibit Norman and French Rural influences on this rambling retreat; see page 57. OPPOSITE BELOW: A rustic stacked-stone surround and chimney echo the ashlar stonework of this home's English Norman exterior; see page 27.

Photo by Ron Kerr, Kerr Studios

high and made from a variety of exterior materials, these small country homes feature high, steep roofs with large chimneys and with dormers breaking through the cornice.

Another distinctive French style—or is it English?—is Norman, brought to England by the French invasion of 1066. Usually one to two stories in height, these houses are asymmetrical with large chimneys and high, complicated roofs. They may be decorated with half timbers and may feature a central turret that contains a staircase. The origin of the turret is interesting: in the beginning, the house and barn were one building and grain or ensilage was stored in the turret.

Tudor is a much older style, dating from the late 5th Century. These houses are more imposing, even fortress-like.

Although employing some stucco and half timbers, they were more often of stone and brick, with high, prominent chimneys topped by chimney pots, and often featuring three-sided bays and turrets. Windows were casement style with leaded glass, often diamond-shaped, and with molded cement or stone trim, mullions and transoms.

Designs from the Mediterranean are very different from those of France and England, featuring large arches, both inside and out, and an abundance of windows. Look for wrought-iron exterior decorations rather than the stickwork of their northern neighbors, and a single exterior material rather than a combination.

The Italian villa is typically a massive two- or three-story house built of masonry, with large overhanging eaves supported by brackets. Many have square or octagonal towers and corner quoins. A Spanish villa has painted stucco exterior walls, a red tile roof and oval-topped windows and doors. A patio completely enclosed by exterior walls is common.

Photo courtesy of Living Concepts Home Planning

Stone Pond

Stone pillars, half-round transoms and a bold turret announce a French Rural influence on this charming style. Lovely stucco columns and a copper standing-seam roof link the revival elements with a modern disposition. An elegant New World interior starts with a sensational winding staircase, a carved handrail and honey-hued hardwood floor. The gallery hall curves gracefully around the staircase and provides a convenient powder room and coat closet for guests

An open two-story formal dining room enjoys front-property views and leads to the gourmet kitchen through the butler's pantry, announced by an archway. Across the foyer, an octagonal formal room easily serves as a library, parlor or den. This room's coffered ceiling and fireplace provide a cozy space to enjoy a good novel or quiet conversation. Beyond the foyer, tall windows brighten the two-story family room and bring in a sense of the outdoors, while a fireplace makes the space cozy and warm. The casual living space opens to the kitchen, which has a walk-in pantry and plenty of counter and cabinet space.

A few steps away, a private vestibule leads to the homeowner's suite through lovely French doors. Built-in bookshelves and a through-fireplace to the bath provide a cozy setting for reading and a kick-your-shoes-off atmosphere that's as welcome as the flowers in May. The second floor includes two family bedrooms that share a full bath. An additional secondary bedroom offers a spacious private bath with a walk-in closet, whirlpool tub and separate shower. A balcony hall lends views to the family room and foyer.

ELEGANT AMENITIES PRESIDE IN THE FORMAL DINING ROOM, A PLACE FOR PLANNED EVENTS AS WELL AS SIMPLE FAMILY MEALS.

Daniel Reedy Interiors

AN OCTAGONAL CEILING, A FIREPLACE
AND BUILT-IN SHELVES AND CABINETRY
LEND A STATELY BUT COMFORTABLE FEEL
TO THE LIBRARY.

STATE-OF-THE-ART APPLIANCES BLEND
EASILY WITH RUSTIC OLD WORLD CHARM
IN THE KITCHEN.

This home, as shown in the photographs, may differ from the actual blueprints. For more detailed information, please check the floor plans carefully.

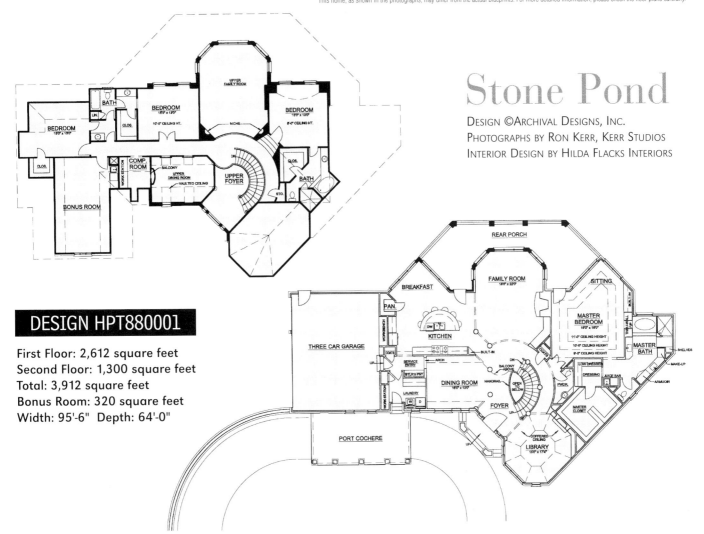

Stone Pond

DESIGN ©ARCHIVAL DESIGNS, INC.
PHOTOGRAPHS BY RON KERR, KERR STUDIOS
INTERIOR DESIGN BY HILDA FLACKS INTERIORS

DESIGN HPT880001

First Floor: 2,612 square feet
Second Floor: 1,300 square feet
Total: 3,912 square feet
Bonus Room: 320 square feet
Width: 95'-6" Depth: 64'-0"

Park Place

Sweet dreams are made of striking architecture, bold lines and a dash of the past. Corinthian columns announce an inviting entry, rich with panels of leaded glass. Marble columns with gilded accents frame a sweeping staircase in the foyer, which opens to the formal dining hall and the grand salon. A bow window brings in plenty of light and a sense of nature, while a massive fireplace anchors this voluminous living space. A vivid palette warms the keeping room and plays counterpoint to natural light and the soothing colors of the peaceful woods outside. Open to the morning nook and kitchen, the keeping room shares the glow of its hearth with the casual eating areas. Well-organized amenities such as an angled cooktop, dual food preparation islands, and a walk-in pantry facilitate even crowd-sized events.

This home, as shown in the photographs, may differ from the actual blueprints. For more detailed information, please check the floor plans carefully.

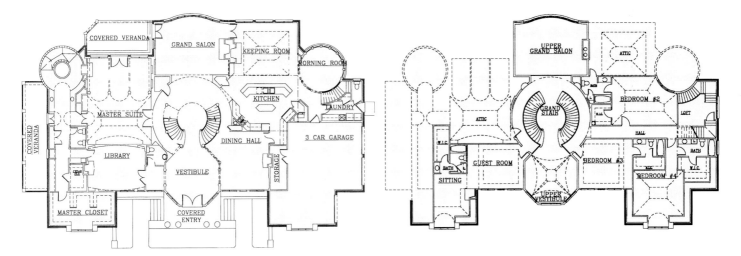

Park Place

DESIGN ©DAVID MARC LOFTUS,
   ARCHIVAL DESIGNS, INC.
BUILDER: RICHARD SULKEN
PHOTOGRAPHS BY RON KERR, KERR STUDIOS
INTERIOR DESIGN BY HILDA FLACKS INTERIORS

DESIGN HPT880002

First Floor: 3,911 square feet
Second Floor: 2,184 square feet
Total: 6,095 square feet
Width: 102'-1" Depth: 62'-5"

Villa de Saye

A subdued facade speaks softly of historic style yet there's nothing shy about this neoclassic villa. Massive Tuscan columns support a five-foot cornice and parapet on this dramatic facade, capped by a copper dome. Twin garages extend the symmetrical footprint as if they were sphinx paws reaching toward the curb. The entry is a spectacular frame for the gallery foyer and grand room. which boasts a coffered ceiling. Interior vistas extend from the front paneled door to the rear loggia and pool, creating a greater sense of spaciousness and light. Intricate details remniscent of antiquities enhance the central salon and allow an historic feeling to pervade this resort-style home. Hand-carved corbels edge the stone fireplace and magnify the elegance of this inside/outside space.

Decorative columns and arches frame the cabinetry that helps to define the formal rooms. A wet bar and counter provide useful accoutrements for planned events.

This home, as shown in the photographs, may differ from the actual blueprints. For more detailed information, please check the floor plans carefully.

Villa de Saye

DESIGN ©ARCHIVAL DESIGNS, INC.
PHOTOGRAPHS BY RON KERR, KERR STUDIOS

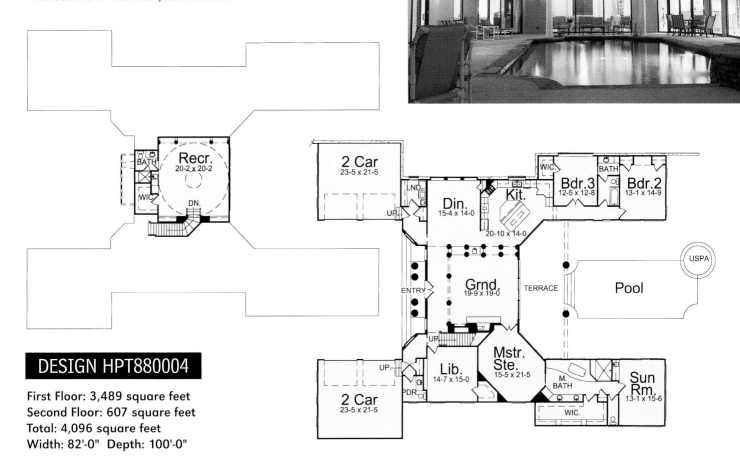

DESIGN HPT880004

First Floor: 3,489 square feet
Second Floor: 607 square feet
Total: 4,096 square feet
Width: 82'-0" Depth: 100'-0"

Recr.
20-2 x 20-2
BATH
WIC
DN.

2 Car
23-5 x 21-5

LND.
UP

Din.
15-4 x 14-0

Kit.

WIC
BATH

Bdr.3
12-5 x 12-8

Bdr.2
13-1 x 14-9

20-10 x 14-0

ENTRY

Grnd.
19-9 x 19-0

TERRACE

Pool

USPA

UP

2 Car
23-5 x 21-5

UP

PDR

Lib.
14-7 x 15-0

Mstr.
Ste.
15-5 x 21-5

M.
BATH

Sun
Rm.
13-1 x 15-6

WIC

Manderleigh

Rows of windows and an enchanting solarium fill these rooms with sunlight and a sense of the outdoors. Grand columns announce a covered terrace, which leads to the foyer through three sets of French doors. At the heart of the home, the grand room features a tray ceiling and a fireplace with a faux-marble surround. Decorative columns and gentle arches announce the great solarium, which extends an invitation to enjoy the rambling entertainment terrace through lovely French doors. An elegant fireplace warms the formal dining room. Plenty of amenities highlight the gourmet kitchen, including a cooktop island counter, planning space and a breakfast area bright with windows. This home is designed with a walkout basement foundation.

EARTHY HUES EMBRACE MODERN APPLIANCES IN THE KITCHEN, WHICH FEATURES AN ARCH-TOPPED WINDOW.

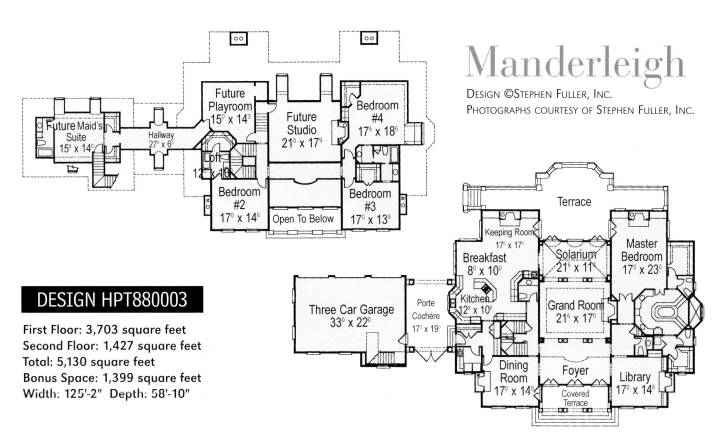

Manderleigh

DESIGN ©STEPHEN FULLER, INC.
PHOTOGRAPHS COURTESY OF STEPHEN FULLER, INC.

Second Floor plan labels:
Future Maid's Suite 15⁰ x 14⁰
Hallway 27⁰ x 6⁰
Future Playroom 15⁰ x 14³
Loft 12⁰ x 10⁰
Future Studio 21⁰ x 17⁹
Bedroom #4 17⁶ x 18⁶
Bedroom #2 17⁰ x 14⁶
Open To Below
Bedroom #3 17⁰ x 13⁰

First Floor plan labels:
Three Car Garage 33⁰ x 22⁰
Porte Cochère 17³ x 19⁰
Terrace
Keeping Room 17⁰ x 17⁰
Breakfast 8⁰ x 10⁰
Kitchen 12⁰ x 10⁰
Solarium 21⁶ x 11⁰
Grand Room 21⁶ x 17⁰
Master Bedroom 17⁰ x 23⁰
Dining Room 17⁰ x 14⁹
Foyer
Covered Terrace
Library 17⁰ x 14⁶

DESIGN HPT880003

First Floor: 3,703 square feet
Second Floor: 1,427 square feet
Total: 5,130 square feet
Bonus Space: 1,399 square feet
Width: 125'-2" Depth: 58'-10"

This home, as shown in the photographs, may differ from the actual blueprints. For more detailed information, please check the floor plans carefully.

Deluxe Whirlpool Bath

DESIGN HPT880200

Stunning Mediterranean style gives this home a sense of palatial elegance. Arches frame the portico, which leads inside to an impressive two-story foyer—a study warmed by a fireplace is to the left, while a formal dining room is introduced to the right. The first-floor master suite enjoys a deluxe whirlpool bath and two walk-in closets. The island kitchen opens to the casual family room, warmed by a second fireplace. Four additional suites reside upstairs for other family members. A romantic overlook views the great room and foyer. A sitting room is placed just outside of the second-floor recreation room.

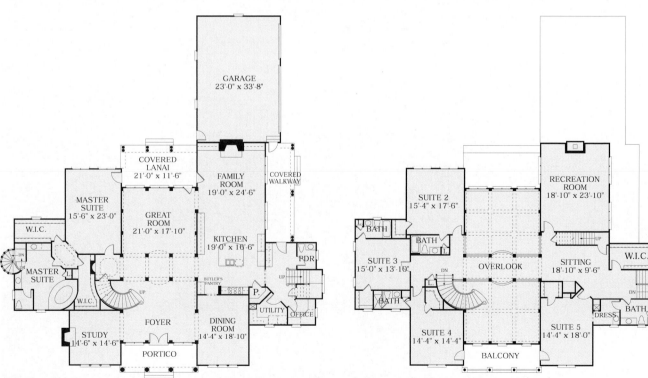

First Floor: 3,592 square feet
Second Floor: 2,861 square feet
Total: 6,453 square feet

Width: 96'-5" Depth: 91'-6"

DESIGN HPT880201

Old World Charm

The ornamental stucco detailing on this home creates an Old World charm. The two-story foyer with a sweeping curved stair opens to the large formal dining room and study. The master suite, offering convenient access to the study, is complete with a fireplace, two walk-in closets and a bath with twin vanities and a separate shower and tub. The two-story great room over-

looks the rear patio. A large kitchen with an island workstation opens to an octagonal-shaped breakfast room and the family room. A staircase located off the family room provides additional access to the three second-floor bedrooms that each offer walk-in closets and plenty of storage. This home is designed with a walk-out basement foundation.

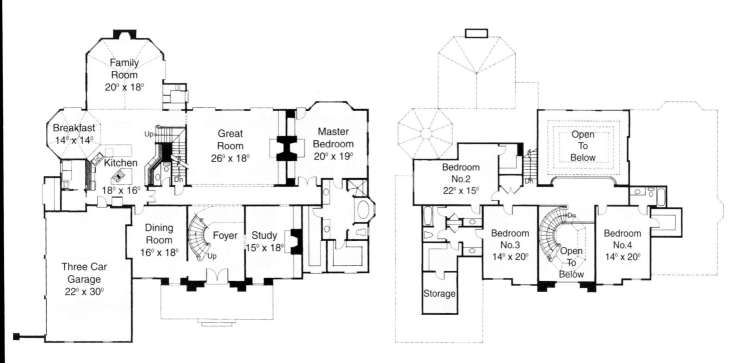

First Floor: 3,568 square feet
Second Floor: 1,667 square feet
Total: 5,235 square feet

Width: 86'-8" **Depth:** 79'-0"

Up-to-date Amenities

This home features two levels of pampering luxury filled with the most up-to-date amenities. Touches of Mediterranean detail add to the striking facade. A wrapping front porch welcomes you inside to a formal dining room and two-story great room warmed by a fireplace. Double doors from the master suite, great room and breakfast nook access the rear veranda. The first-floor master suite enjoys a luxury bath, roomy walk-in closet and close access to the front-facing office/study. Three additional bedrooms reside upstairs. Please specify basement or slab foundation when ordering.

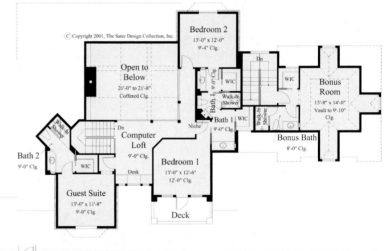

First Floor: 2,222 square feet
Second Floor: 1,075 square feet
Total: 3,297 square feet

Width: 91'-0" Depth: 52'-8"

DESIGN HPT880006

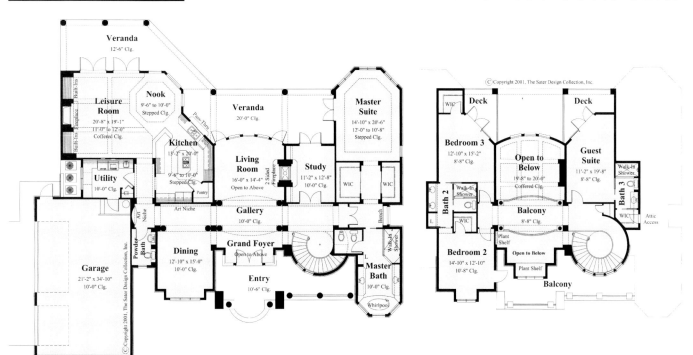

M editerranean accents enhance the facade of this contemporary estate home. Two fanciful turret bays add a sense of grandeur to the exterior. Double doors open inside to a grand two-story foyer. A two-sided fireplace warms the study and two-story living room. The master suite is found to the right and includes a private bath, two walk-in closets and double-door access to sweeping rear veranda. Casual areas of the home include the gourmet island kitchen, breakfast nook and leisure room warmed by a fireplace. A spiral staircase leads upstairs, where a second-floor balcony separates two family bedrooms from the luxurious guest suite.

First Floor: 2,829 square feet
Second Floor: 1,127 square feet
Total: 3,956 square feet

Width: 85'-0" Depth: 76'-2"

19

This home, as shown in the photograph, may differ from the actual blueprints. For more detailed information, please check the floor plans carefully.
Photo by Living Concepts Home Planning

Large Gathering Room

The grand exterior of this Normandy country design features a steep-pitch gable roofline. Arched dormers repeat the window accents. Inside, the promise of space is fulfilled with a large gathering room that fills the center of the house and opens to a long trellised veranda. The den or guest suite with a fireplace, the adjacent powder room and the master suite with a vaulted ceiling and access to the veranda are in the right wing. Two additional bedrooms with two baths and a loft overlooking the gathering room are upstairs. A large bonus room is found over the garage. It can be developed later as office or hobby space.

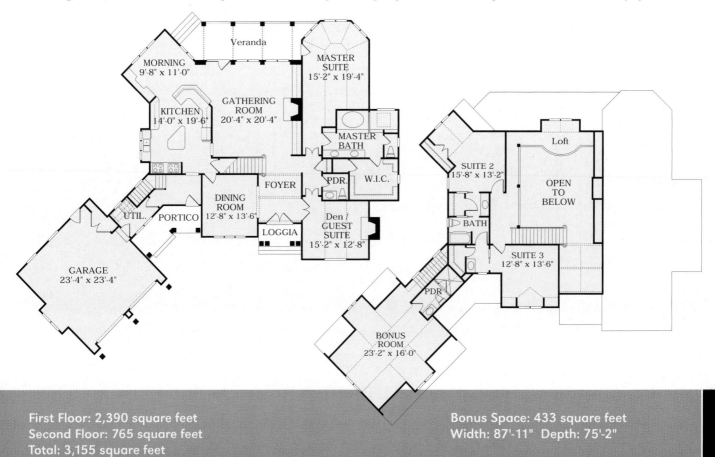

First Floor: 2,390 square feet
Second Floor: 765 square feet
Total: 3,155 square feet

Bonus Space: 433 square feet
Width: 87'-11" Depth: 75'-2"

DESIGN HPT880008

Graced with Amenities

Accommodate your life's diverse pattern of formal occasions and casual times with this spacious home. The exterior of this estate presents a palatial bearing, while the interior is both comfortable and elegant. Formal areas are graced with amenities to make entertaining easy. Casual areas are kept intimate, but no less large. The solarium serves both with skylights and terrace access. Guests will appreciate a private guest room and a bath with loggia access on the first floor.

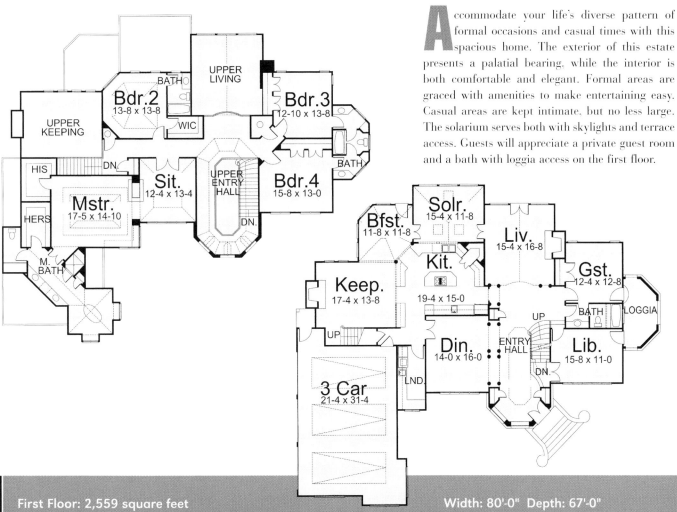

First Floor: 2,559 square feet
Second Floor: 2,140 square feet
Total: 4,699 square feet

Width: 80'-0" Depth: 67'-0"

21

This home, as shown in the photograph, may differ from the actual blueprints. For more detailed information, please check the floor plans carefully.
Photo by Frank Grillo

Commanding Presence

This European-style, brick-and-stucco home showcases an arched entry and presents a commanding presence from the curb. Inside, the living room, the dining room and the family room are located at the rear of the home to provide wide-open views of the rear grounds beyond. A colonnade with connecting arches defines the space for a living room with a fireplace and the dining room. The spacious master suite features a relaxing sitting area, His and Hers closets and an extravagant bath. Take special note of the private His and Hers bathrooms. On the second floor, three bedrooms, two baths and a game room complete the home.

Quote One®

Cost to build? See page 214
to order complete cost estimate
to build this house in your area!

First Floor: 2,188 square feet
Second Floor: 1,110 square feet
Total: 3,298 square feet

Width: 69'-0" Depth: 64'-8"

L

DESIGN HPT880202

Cozy Sanctuary

Quaint, yet as majestic as a country manor on the Rhine, this European-style stucco home enjoys the enchantment of arched windows to underscore its charm. The two-story foyer leads through French doors to the study with its own hearth and coffered ceiling. Coupled with this cozy sanctuary is the master suite with a tray ceiling and large accommodating bath. The large sunken great room is highlighted by a fireplace, built-in bookcases, lots of glass and easy access to a back stair and large gourmet kitchen. Three secondary bedrooms reside upstairs. One spacious upstairs bedroom gives guests the ultimate in convenience with a private bath and walk-in closet. This home is designed with a walkout basement foundation.

First Floor: 2,208 square feet
Second Floor: 1,250 square feet
Total: 3,458 square feet

Width: 60'-6" Depth: 60'-0"

Country French Estate

DESIGN HPT880011

The European character of this home is enhanced through the use of stucco and stone on the exterior, giving this country French estate home its charm and beauty. The foyer leads to the dining room and study/living room. The two-story family room is positioned for convenient access to the back staircase, kitchen, wet bar and deck area. The master bedroom is privately located on the right side of the home with an optional entry to the study and a large garden bath. Upstairs, two secondary bedrooms share a full bath, while a guest suite provides rich amenities. This home is designed with a walkout basement foundation.

First Floor: 2,346 square feet
Second Floor: 1,260 square feet
Total: 3,606 square feet

Width: 68'-11" Depth: 58'-9"

DESIGN HPT880010

Lovely Bay Windows

QUOTE ONE®
Cost to build? See page 214
to order complete cost estimate
to build this house in your area!

A perfect blend of stucco and stacked stone sets off keystones, transoms and arches in this French country facade to inspire an elegant spirit. The foyer is flanked by the spacious dining room and the study, accented by a vaulted ceiling and a fireplace. A great room with a full wall of glass connects the interior with the outdoors. A first-floor master suite offers both style and intimacy with a coffered ceiling and a secluded bath. This home is designed with a walkout basement foundation.

First Floor: 1,900 square feet
Second Floor: 800 square feet
Total: 2,700 square feet

Width: 63'-0" **Depth:** 51'-0"

Varied Window Treatments

Rich with Old World elements, this English country manor steps sweetly into the future with great rooms and splendid outdoor spaces. Varied window treatments define this elegant facade, enhanced by a massive stone turret. A leaded-glass paneled door with sidelights leads to a gallery-style foyer. Grand interior vistas are provided by a soaring triple window capped with an arch-top transom. The living area leads to the breakfast bay and gourmet kitchen. This culinary paradise features a food-preparation island and a peninsula snack counter. Double doors open to a quiet library with a turret-style bay window. The master retreat boasts views of the secluded side property.

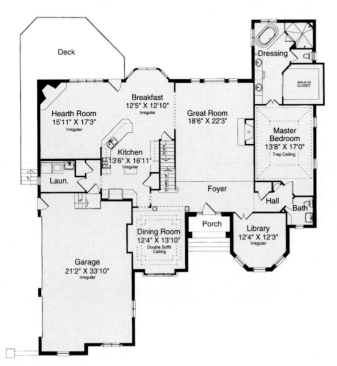

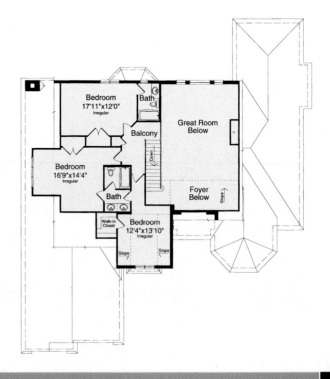

First Floor: 2,479 square feet
Second Floor: 956 square feet
Total: 3,435 square feet

Width: 67'-6" Depth: 75'-6"

DESIGN HPT880012

Panoramic View

If you've ever traveled the European countryside, past rolling hills that range in hue from apple-green to deep, rich emerald, you may have come upon a home much like this one. Stone accents combined with stucco, and shutters that frame multi-pane windows add a touch of charm that introduces the marvelous floor plan found inside. The foyer opens onto a great room that offers a panoramic view of the veranda and beyond. To the left, you'll find a formal dining room; to the right, a quiet den. Just steps away resides the sitting room that introduces the grand master suite.

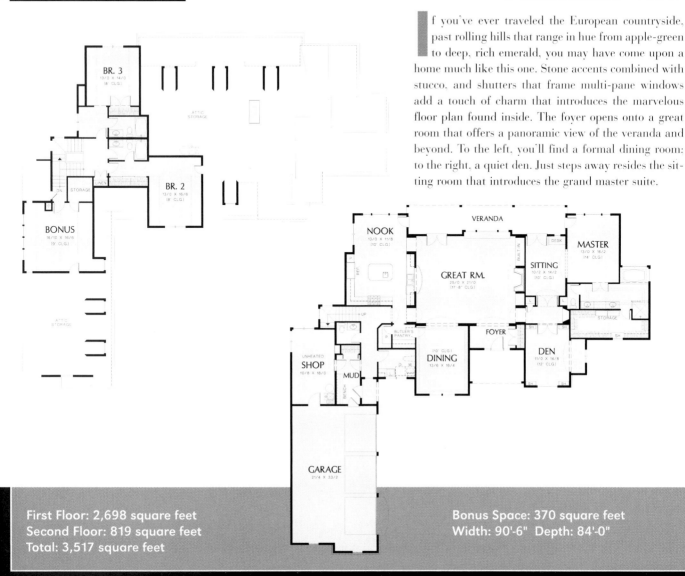

First Floor: 2,698 square feet
Second Floor: 819 square feet
Total: 3,517 square feet

Bonus Space: 370 square feet
Width: 90'-6" **Depth:** 84'-0"

This home, as shown in the photograph, may differ from the actual blueprints. For more detailed information, please check the floor plans carefully.
Photo by Living Concepts Home Planning

Special Details

Stickwork, dormers, shutters and an unusual balustrade planter area are special details on this French-style stucco exterior. Inside, a large open area includes the family room, kitchen and breakfast area. Family and friends will enjoy the massive fireplace and easy access to the covered terrace, while the resident chef will appreciate the island cooktop and the walk-in pantry. A good-sized laundry is nearby, as is the formal dining room, which boasts a second fireplace. Each of the home's four bedrooms boasts a private bath and a walk-in closet. The master suite also contains a retreat with a fireplace.

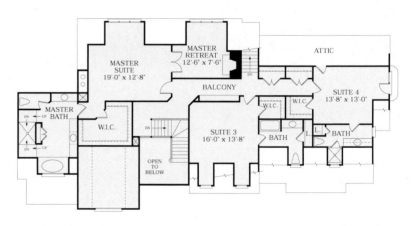

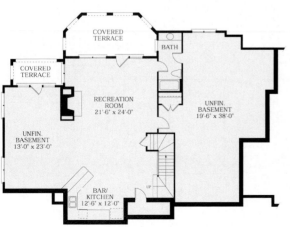

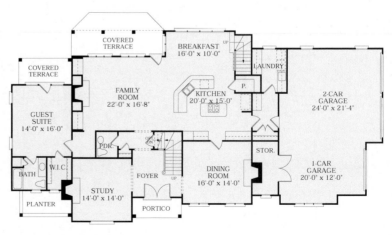

First Floor: 2,124 square feet
Second Floor: 1,962 square feet
Total: 4,086 square feet

Finished Basement: 1,295 square feet
Width: 88'-0" Depth: 48'-0"

DESIGN HPT880015

Tudor Adaptation

Here is truly an exquisite Tudor adaptation. The exterior could hardly be more dramatic, with its interesting roof lines, window treatment, stately chimney and appealing use of brick and stucco. Inside, the delightfully large receiving hall has a two-story ceiling and controls the flexible traffic patterns. The living and dining rooms, with the library nearby, will cater to for-mal living pursuits. The guest room offers another haven for the enjoyment of peace and quiet. The casual living space offers a raised-hearth fireplace, built-in bar and the kitchen pass-through. Adding to the charm of the family room is its high ceiling. The second floor offers three family bedrooms, a lounge and a deluxe master suite.

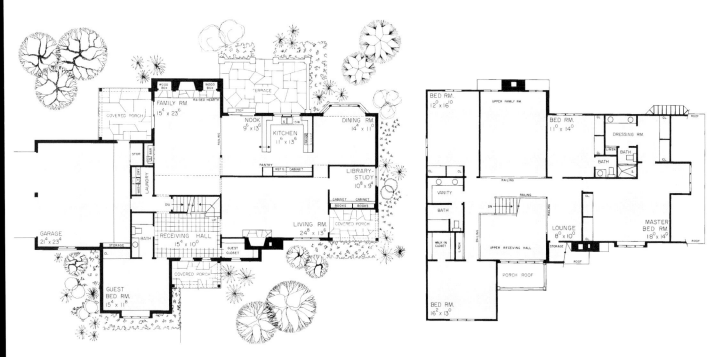

First Floor: 1,969 square feet
Second Floor: 1,702 square feet
Total: 3,671 square feet

Width: 79'-10"   Depth: 53'-6"

Spacious Gathering Room

DESIGN HPT880014

Attractive stone, curved dormers and varied rooflines give this fine European manor a graceful dose of class. Inside, the foyer introduces a formal dining room defined by columns and a spacious gathering room with a fireplace. The nearby kitchen features a walk-in pantry, beamed ceiling, adjacent breakfast nook and a screened porch. The first-floor master suite features two walk-in closets, a lavish bath, a corner fireplace and a sitting room with access to the rear veranda. Upstairs, three suites offer walk-in closets and surround a study loft. On the lower level, a huge recreation room awaits to entertain with a bar, a fireplace and outdoor access. A secluded office provides a private entrance—perfect for a home business.

First Floor: 2,734 square feet
Second Floor: 1,605 square feet
Total: 4,339 square feet

Bonus Space: 391 square feet
Finished Basement: 1,701 square feet
Width: 88'-0" Depth: 92'-8"

DESIGN HPT880016

Numerous Amenities

The distinctive covered entry to this stunning manor, flanked by twin turrets, leads to a gracious foyer with impressive fanlights. The plan opens from the foyer to a formal dining room, a study and a step-down gathering room. The spacious kitchen has numerous amenities, including an island work station and a built-in desk. The adjacent morning room and the gathering room, with a wet bar and a raised-hearth fireplace, are bathed in light and open to the terrace for outdoor entertaining. The luxurious and secluded master suite includes two walk-in closets, a dressing area and an exercise area with a spa.

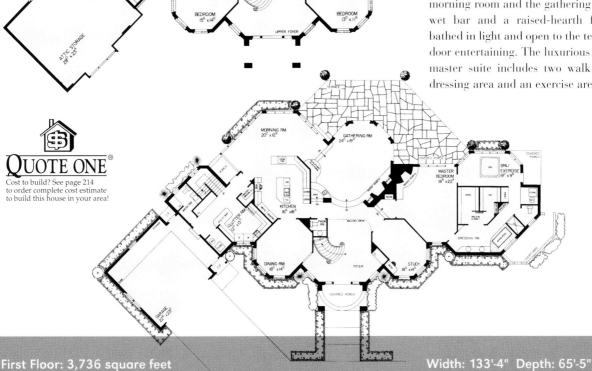

QUOTE ONE®
Cost to build? See page 214
to order complete cost estimate
to build this house in your area!

First Floor: 3,736 square feet
Second Floor: 2,264 square feet
Total: 6,000 square feet

Width: 133'-4" Depth: 65'-5"

L

Expansive Rear Views

DESIGN HPT880017

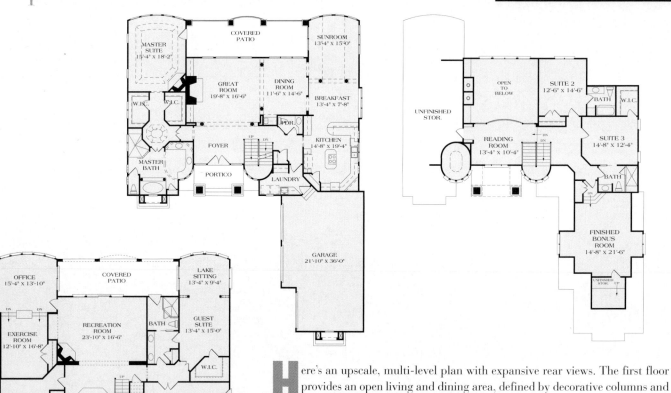

H ere's an upscale, multi-level plan with expansive rear views. The first floor provides an open living and dining area, defined by decorative columns and enhanced by natural light from tall windows. A breakfast area with a love-ly triple window opens to a sun room, which allows light to pour into the gourmet kitchen. The master wing features a tray ceiling in the bedroom, two walk-in clos-ets and an elegant private vestibule leading to a lavish bath. Upstairs, a reading loft overlooks the great room and leads to a sleeping area with two suites.

First Floor: 2,391 square feet
Second Floor: 922 square feet
Total: 3,313 square feet

Bonus Space: 400 square feet
Finished Basement: 1,964 square feet
Width: 63'-10" Depth: 85'-6"

Homes with a French Flair

To view floor plans, see page 24.

Spacious Family Room

Triple dormers highlight the roofline of this distinctive single-level French country design. Double doors enhance the covered entryway, which leads to a grand open area with graceful columns outlining the dimensions of the formal living room and dining room. The large family room with a fireplace leads through double doors to the rear terrace. An L-shaped island kitchen opens to a breakfast area with a bay window. The master suite fills one wing and features a bay window, vaulted ceilings and access to the terrace. Two additional bedrooms on the opposite side of the house share a full bath.

Square Footage: 2,500

Width: 73'-0" Depth: 65'-10"

Photo courtesy of Living Concepts Home Planning
This home, as shown in the photograph, may differ from the actual blueprints. For more detailed information, please check the floor plans carefully.

DESIGN HPT880020

Two Additional Suites

European formality meets a bold American spirit in this splendid transitional plan. Perfect for a lake or golf course setting, this home offers walls of windows in the living areas. Soak up the scenery in the sun room, which opens from the breakfast nook and leads to a rear terrace or deck. Ten-foot ceilings throughout the main level provide interior vistas and add volume to the rooms. The library features a tray ceiling and an arched window, and would make an excellent home office or guest suite. Classical columns divide the great room and dining room, which has a see-through wet bar. The deluxe master suite uses defining columns between the bedroom and the lavish bath and walk-in closet. Upstairs, there are two additional suites and a bonus room. Please specify basement or crawlspace foundation when ordering.

First Floor: 2,398 square feet
Second Floor: 657 square feet
Total: 3,055 square feet

Bonus Room: 374 square feet
Width: 72'-8" Depth: 69'-1"

Romantic Upstairs Balcony

The stately contemporary proportions and exquisite Mediterranean detailing of this home are sure to please. Like so many European houses, interesting rooflines set the character of this design. Observe the delightful interplay of the gable roof, hipped roof and front turrets. A sturdy brick exterior is offset by delicate window detailing, railings and a romantic upstairs balcony above the front entry. Inside is a very livable plan. The kitchen features a circular breakfast counter for casual dining and an adjoining formal dining area. A splendid staircase leads upstairs to the sleeping area, which contains a well-appointed master suite plus two family bedrooms that share a full bath. This home is designed with a basement foundation.

First Floor: 1,468 square feet
Second Floor: 936 square feet
Total: 2,404 square feet

Width: 54'-0" Depth: 44'-0"

DESIGN HPT880022

Two-Story Turret

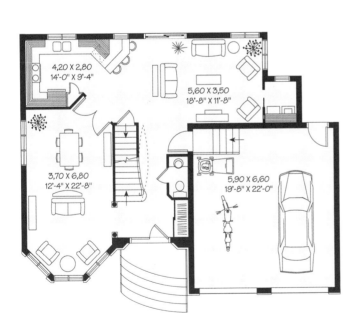

4,20 X 2,80
14'-0" X 9'-4"

5,60 X 3,50
18'-8" X 11'-8"

3,70 X 6,80
12'-4" X 22'-8"

5,90 X 6,60
19'-8" X 22'-0"

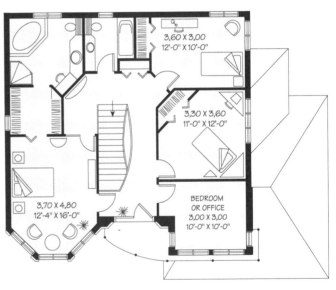

3,60 X 3,00
12'-0" X 10'-0"

3,30 X 3,60
11'-0" X 12'-0"

3,70 X 4,80
12'-4" X 16'-0"

BEDROOM
OR OFFICE
3,00 X 3,00
10'-0" X 10'-0"

This magnificent European adaptation is highlighted by hipped roofs, plenty of windows, cornice detailing and an elegant entrance door adjacent to an impressive two-story turret. Inside are a magnificent living/dining area, U-shaped kitchen, breakfast bar and comfortable family room. A gracious staircase leads upstairs to a deluxe master suite lavish in its efforts to pamper you. A well-lit home office and two secondary bedrooms share this level with a full bath. This home is designed with a basement foundation.

First Floor: 924 square feet
Second Floor: 1,052 square feet
Total: 1,976 square feet

Width: 44'-8" Depth: 36'-0"

Circular Staircase

DESIGN HPT880023

The steeply pitched hipped roof with dormers atop this stone and stucco facade offer a feeling of the Old English countryside. The formal dining room resides to the right of the grand foyer where the circular staircase creates a magnificent first impression. The great room is defined by three arches in the gallery which leads to the master suite on the left and the kitchen on the right. Beyond the island kitchen lies the family room with its fireplace and built-ins. Fireplaces are also found in the master bedroom, the great room and the study.

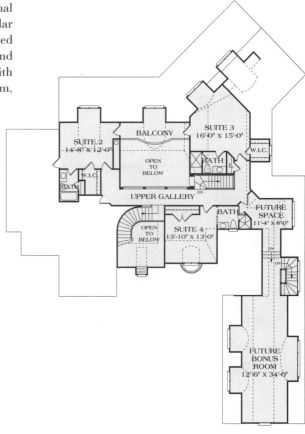

First Floor: 3,389 square feet
Second Floor: 1,358 square feet
Total: 4,747 square feet

Bonus Space: 805 square feet
Width: 82'-7" Depth: 109'-6"

DESIGN HPT880024

Two-Story Pool House

Amenities abound in this opulent French Country design, which includes a separate apartment or guest house and a two-story pool house. Entertaining is easy, with a central grand room and the formal dining room located right off the foyer. The heart of your gatherings, though, will be in the combination kitchen, breakfast nook and gathering room, where a fireplace and a private screened porch make this area warm and comfortable. Another favorite area will be the upper-level recreation room that opens, via French doors, to a home theater with a platform. While the sumptuous master suite is located on the first floor for privacy, four guest suites are available on the second floor. A skylit loft is tucked away on the third floor.

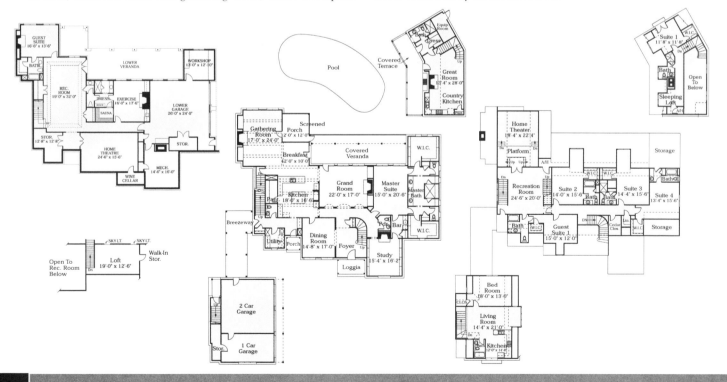

First Floor: 3,880 square feet
Second Floor: 3,317 square feet
Total: 7,197 square feet

Finished Basement: 2,531 square feet
Width: 101'-4" Depth: 110'-4"

Private Garden with Fountain

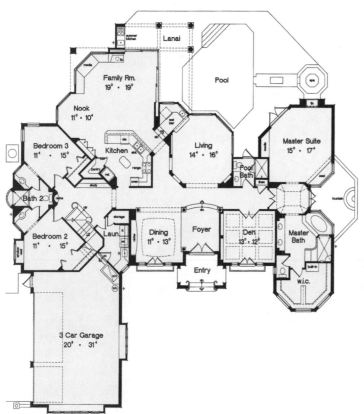

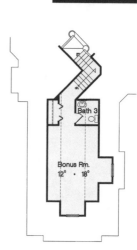

From a more graceful era, this 1½-story estate evokes the sense of quiet refinement. Exquisite exterior detailing makes it a one-of-a-kind. Inside are distinctive treatments that make the floor plan unique and functional. The central foyer is enhanced with columns that define the dining room and formal living room. A beam ceiling complements the den. An indulgent master suite includes a private garden with a fountain, pool access, a large walk-in closet and a fireplace to the outdoor spa. Family bedrooms share an unusual compartmented bath. The kitchen and family room are completed with a breakfast nook. Pool access and a lanai with a summer kitchen make this area a natural for casual lifestyles. A bonus area over the garage can become a home office or game room.

Square Footage: 3,064
Bonus Room: 366 square feet

Width: 79'-6" Depth: 91'-0"

DESIGN HPT880026

Deluxe Master Bath

This captivating European manor speaks all the romance of the Old World. The right wing of the home is devoted to the master suite, which provides a deluxe master bath and double walk-in closet. The dining and gathering rooms combine for easy entertaining and open to the rear terrace and screened porch. The kitchen is opposite to a large pantry and faces the hearth-warmed den. The second floor includes a guest suite, an exercise room and unfinished space to be used as the family grows. The basement level adds luxury to exquisite planning with room for a spa and wine cellar.

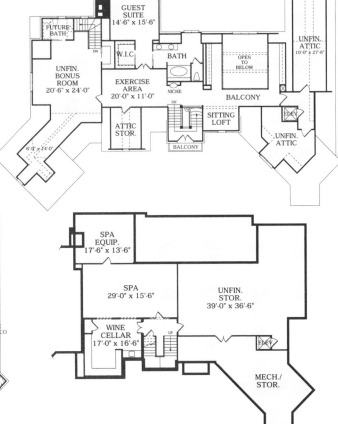

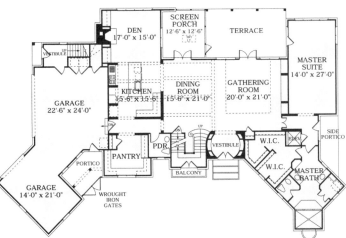

First Floor: 2,911 square feet
Second Floor: 1,345 square feet
Total: 4,256 square feet

Bonus Space: 721 square feet
Finished Basement: 857 square feet
Width: 107'-1"   **Depth:** 67'-7"

Chateau Style

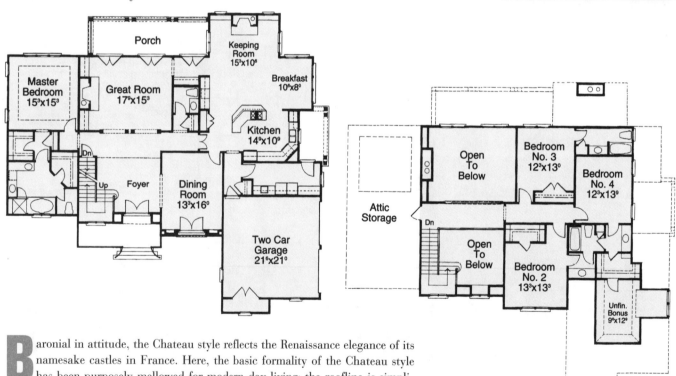

B aronial in attitude, the Chateau style reflects the Renaissance elegance of its namesake castles in France. Here, the basic formality of the Chateau style has been purposely mellowed for modern-day living: the roofline is simplified, and massive masonry construction is replaced by a stucco finish. However, none of the drama has been lost in the translation. The two-story foyer is made for grand entrances, with a marble floor and a sweeping staircase. The foyer opens to the formal dining room and leads to the great room with its fireplace, vaulted ceiling and wet bar. This home is designed with a walkout basement foundation.

First Floor: 2,357 square feet
Second Floor: 1,021 square feet
Total: 3,378 square feet

Bonus Room: 168 square feet
Width: 70'-0" Depth: 62'-6"

Stunning Sitting Bay

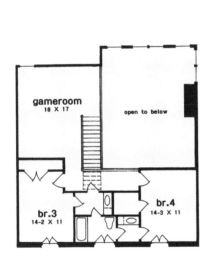

The symmetrical front of this home conceals an imaginatively asymmetrical floor plan beyond. A keeping room, a sitting area in the master bedroom and a second bedroom all jut out from this home, forming interesting angles and providing extra window space. Two fireplaces, a game room, a study, and His and Hers bathrooms in the master suite are interesting elements in this home. The bayed kitchen, with a walk-in pantry and a center island with room for seating, is sure to lure guests and family alike. The open floor plan and two-story ceilings in the family room add a contemporary touch.

First Floor: 2,780 square feet
Second Floor: 878 square feet
Total: 3,658 square feet

Bonus Room: 206 square feet
Width: 68'-3" Depth: 89'-1"

Guest Suite

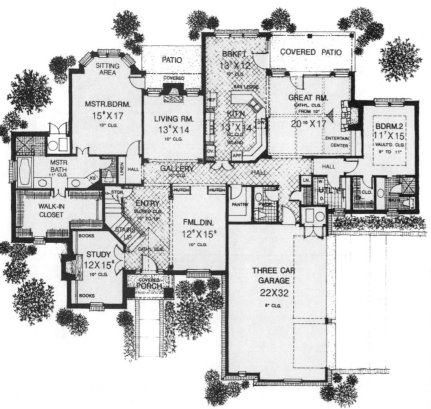

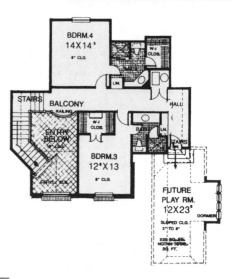

This dazzling and majestic European design features a stucco and stone facade, French shutters and castle-like rooflines. The entry is flanked by a study with a fireplace and a formal dining room. A formal living room with a fireplace is just across the gallery. The master wing is brightened by a bayed sitting area and features a private bath that extends impressive closet space. The island kitchen overlooks the breakfast and great rooms. A guest suite is located on the first floor for privacy, while two additional family bedrooms reside upstairs, along with a future playroom.

First Floor: 3,030 square feet
Second Floor: 848 square feet
Total: 3,878 square feet

Bonus Space: 320 square feet
Width: 88'-0" Depth: 72'-1"

I n the Pays Basque region of rural France, you can find finished farmhouses such as this beauty. The steeply pitched roof drains water quickly, and the curved eaves push the water away from the wall, protecting the stucco. The two-story entry is graced with a beautiful curved stair, opening to a two-story living room with a vaulted ceiling. To the right is a formal dining room and to the left, a finely detailed library with a vaulted ceiling and an impressive arched window. The private master suite, with its vaulted ceiling, king-size bath and huge walk-in closets, will never go out of style.

First Floor: 3,182 square feet
Second Floor: 1,190 square feet
Total: 4,372 square feet

Width: 104'-0" Depth: 60'-0"

Comfortable Family Gatherings

European hospitality comes to mind with this home's high hipped roof, arched dormers and welcoming front porch. This clever and original two-story plan begins with the foyer opening to the staircase. At the end of the foyer, a spacious great room provides built-ins, a warming fireplace and double doors leading to the deck. The kitchen has excellent accommodations for preparation of meals, and the keeping room (with access to the deck) will make family gatherings comfortable. Note the storage space, powder room and pantry near the two-car garage. Inside the master suite, an enormous walk-in closet divides the bath, with its own shower, garden tub and double-bowl vanity.

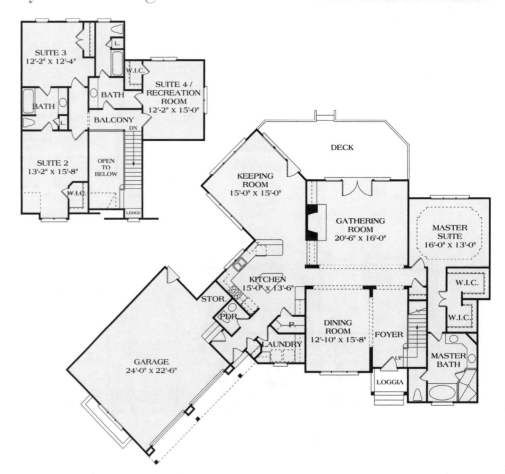

First Floor: 2,060 square feet
Second Floor: 926 square feet
Total: 2,986 square feet

Width: 86'-0" Depth: 65'-5"

DESIGN HPT880032

Spacious Family Room

Elegant hipped rooflines, fine brick detailing and arches galore combine to give this home a wonderful touch of French class. Inside, the two-story foyer is flanked by the formal living and dining rooms, while casual living takes place at the rear of the home. Here, a spacious family room features a fireplace, access to a screened porch and an adjacent breakfast area. The C-shaped kitchen offers a cooktop island and a walk-in pantry. Secluded for privacy, the first-floor master suite includes two walk-in closets, a lavish bath and a sitting area. Upstairs, four suites provide walk-in closets and share two full baths.

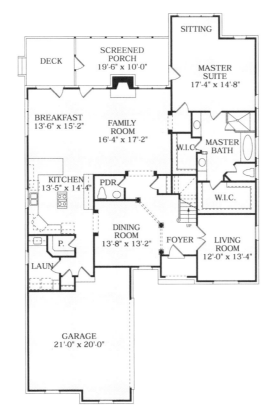

First Floor: 2,080 square feet
Second Floor: 1,362 square feet
Total: 3,442 square feet

Width: 44'-9" Depth: 79'-6"

Floor-to-ceiling Windows

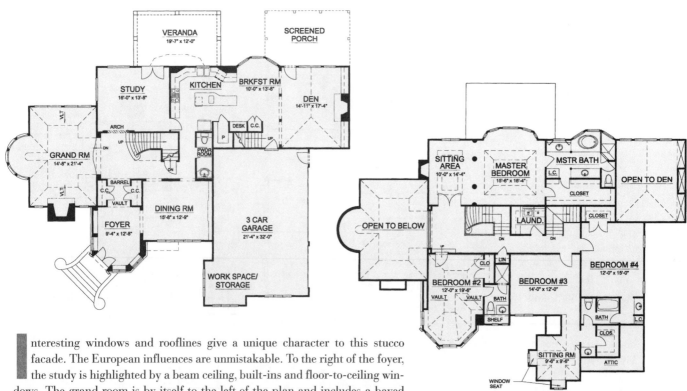

Interesting windows and rooflines give a unique character to this stucco facade. The European influences are unmistakable. To the right of the foyer, the study is highlighted by a beam ceiling, built-ins and floor-to-ceiling windows. The grand room is by itself to the left of the plan and includes a bayed sitting area and a fireplace. Another bay window brightens the breakfast room, which is found between the island kitchen and a den with a second fireplace. The living room and a grand stair hall complete the first floor. The elegant stairway leads up to three family bedrooms and a sumptuous master suite.

First Floor: 2,007 square feet
Second Floor: 1,959 square feet
Total: 3,966 square feet

Width: 77'-0" Depth: 52'-0"

DESIGN HPT880034

Hearth-Warmed Master Bedroom

This stucco-and-stone chateau offers five bedrooms and a second-floor activity room within a European facade. Two front towers hold the formal dining room and a study on the first floor and two family bedrooms on the second floor. The great room is at the back of the plan and features sliding doors to the rear terrace and a cozy hearth. The master bedroom is also hearth-warmed and is graced by a sitting room and a master bath with two walk-in closets. Casual gatherings occur in the kitchen/morning room, which features an island work center.

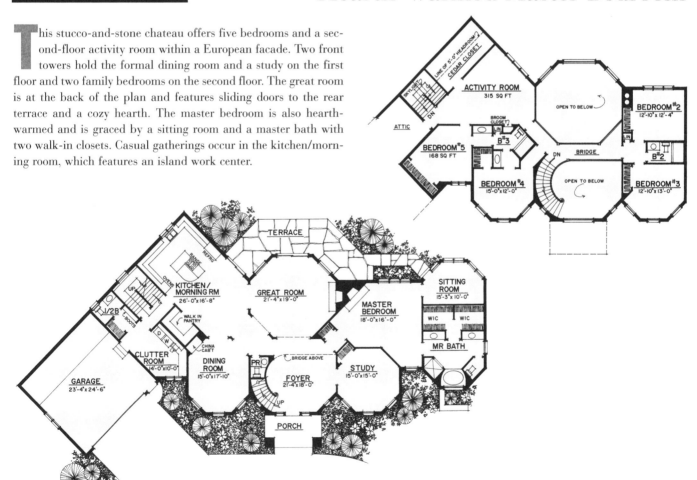

First Floor: 2,960 square feet
Second Floor: 1,729 square feet
Total: 4,689 square feet

Width: 117'-4" Depth: 59'-3"

Splendid Entry

A high, hip roof, towering turret and splendid entrance set the tone for this elegant plan. The grand foyer has an eleven-foot ceiling which opens to the sunlit formal dining room and cathedral great room with fireplace. The gourmet kitchen with cooking island is open to a bayed breakfast area and to a deck outside for informal dining and relaxing. The master bedroom suite enjoys a private bath, dual lavs, a shower and compartmented toilet and His and Hers walk-in closets.

Square Footage: 2,027   Width: 80'-2" Depth: 61'-0"

DESIGN HPT880036

Vaulted Family Room

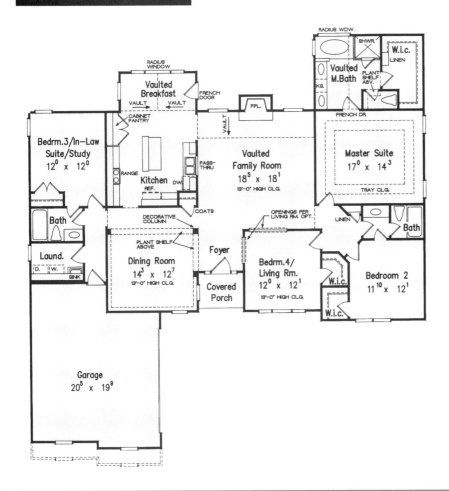

RADIUS WINDOW

Vaulted Breakfast

VAULT | VAULT

FRENCH DOOR

CABINET PANTRY

Bedrm.3/In–Law Suite/Study
12⁰ x 12⁰

Kitchen

RANGE

REF. | DW

PASS-THRU

Bath

Laund.

D. | W.

SINK

DECORATIVE COLUMN

COATS

PLANT SHELF ABOVE

Dining Room
14³ x 12⁷
13'-0" HIGH CLG.

Foyer

Covered Porch

RADIUS WDW.

SHWR

W.i.c.

LINEN

Vaulted M.Bath

KS.

PLANT SHELF ABV.

FRENCH DR.

FPL.

VAULT

Vaulted Family Room
18⁵ x 18¹
13'-0" HIGH CLG.

Master Suite
17⁰ x 14³

TRAY CLG.

OPENINGS PER LIVING RM. OPT.

LINEN

Bath

Bedrm.4/ Living Rm.
12⁰ x 12¹
13'-0" HIGH CLG.

W.i.c.

Bedroom 2
11¹⁰ x 12¹

W.i.c.

Garage
20⁵ x 19⁹

Arched windows, copper and hipped roofs and a grand entryway all combine to create visual poetry in this three-bedroom home. Inside, the layout is designed for entertaining. The formal dining room—with a plant shelf above—is separated from the vaulted family room, with its warming fireplace, by decorative columns. The large and efficient island kitchen is just steps away. A sunny vaulted breakfast room is available for casual morning meals. The master suite is designed to pamper and offers a tray ceiling, large walk-in closet and vaulted bath. The secondary bedroom located behind the kitchen has a full bath available and can be used as a guest suite. Please specify basement or crawlspace foundation when ordering.

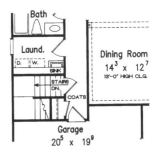

Bath

Laund.

D. | W.

SINK

STAIRS DN.

COATS

Dining Room
14³ x 12⁷
13'-0" HIGH CLG.

Garage
20⁵ x 19⁹

Optional Basement Stair Location

Square Footage: 2,158

Width: 63'-0" Depth: 63'-6"

Large Game Room

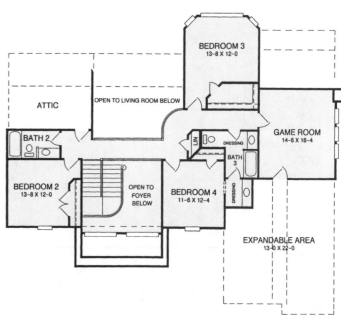

Flower boxes, arches and multi-pane windows all combine to create the elegant facade of this four-bedroom home. Inside, the two-story foyer has a formal dining room to its right and leads to a two-story living room that is filled with light. An efficient kitchen has a bayed breakfast room and shares a snack bar with a cozy family room. Located on the first floor for privacy, the master suite is graced with a luxurious bath. Upstairs, three secondary bedrooms share two full baths and access a large game room. For future growth there is an expandable area accessed through the game room. Please specify basement, crawlspace or slab foundation when ordering.

First Floor: 1,919 square feet
Second Floor: 1,190 square feet
Total: 3,109 square feet

Bonus Space: 286 square feet
Width: 64'-6" Depth: 55'-10"

DESIGN HPT880038

Inviting Facade

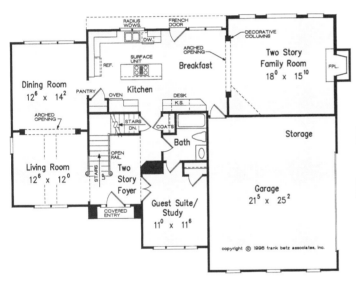

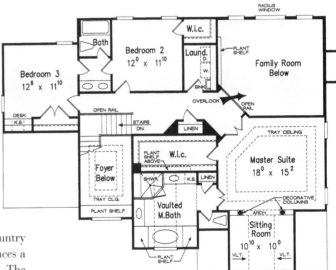

Charming French accents create an inviting facade on this country home. An arched opening set off by decorative columns introduces a two-story family room with a fireplace and a radius window. The gourmet kitchen features an island cooktop counter, a planning desk and a roomy breakfast area with a French door to the back property. The second-floor master suite offers a secluded sitting room, a tray ceiling in the bedroom and a lavish bath with an oversized corner shower. Two family bedrooms share a gallery hall with a balcony overlook to the family room. Please specify basement or crawlspace foundation when ordering.

First Floor: 1,374 square feet
Second Floor: 1,311 square feet
Total: 2,685 square feet

Width: 57'-4"   Depth: 42'-0"

Pleasing Covered Porch

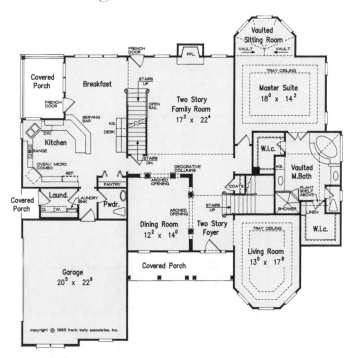

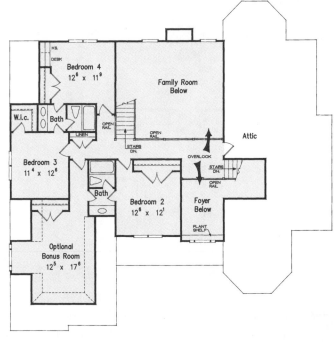

It will be a pleasure to come home to this traditional French design after a long day at work. From the pleasing covered porch, the two-story foyer leads through an arched opening to the formal dining room and also to the charming bayed living room. A convenient stairway leads up to the second floor. The master suite is tucked away on the first floor, with its own vault-ed sitting room, walk-in closet and spacious bath. The two-story family room with a fireplace and rear views rounds out the main level. Three more bedrooms and two baths, plus an optional bonus room (which would be perfect for a home theater), complete the upper level. Please specify basement or crawlspace foundation when ordering.

First Floor: 2,294 square feet
Second Floor: 869 square feet
Total: 3,163 square feet

Bonus Space: 309 square feet
Width: 63'-6" Depth: 63'-0"

© *Stephen Fuller*, Inc.

DESIGN HPT880040

21st-Century Livability

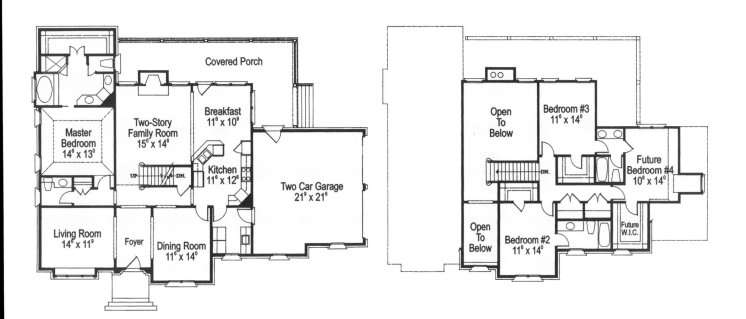

Covered Porch

Breakfast
11⁶ x 10⁹

Two-Story
Family Room
15⁰ x 14⁶

Master
Bedroom
14⁶ x 13⁰

Kitchen
11⁶ x 12⁶

UP   DN.

Two Car Garage
21⁹ x 21⁶

Living Room
14⁶ x 11⁹

Foyer

Dining Room
11⁶ x 14⁰

Open
To
Below

Bedroom #3
11⁶ x 14⁰

Future
Bedroom #4
10⁶ x 14⁰

DN.

Open
To
Below

Bedroom #2
11⁶ x 14⁰

Future
W.I.C.

S tately brick and jack-arch detailing create an exterior with an established look, yet the floor plan offers 21st-Century livability. A dramatic two-story entry is framed by formal living and dining areas. The cheery breakfast nook allows rear covered porch access and opens to a kitchen loaded with modern amenities. A coffered ceiling, His and Hers vanities and a walk-in closet highlight the master suite. Upstairs, Bedroom 2 features a private bath, while Bedroom 3 provides private access to a compartmented bath that's shared with future Bedroom 4. This home is designed with a walkout basement foundation.

QUOTE ONE®
Cost to build? See page 214
to order complete cost estimate
to build this house in your area!

First Floor: 1,660 square feet
Second Floor: 665 square feet
Total: 2,325 square feet

Bonus Space: 240 square feet
Width: 64'-0" Depth: 48'-6"

Tiled Gourmet Kitchen

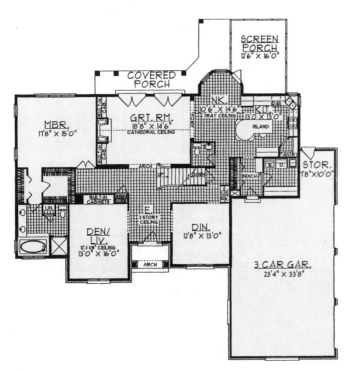

European details highlight this attractive compact exterior. Note the double-brick arches over the windows and entry, the wooden shutters and the stone exterior. The two-story foyer opens to a wide hallway with a coat closet and an elegant stairway. To the left, the den (or living room) features an unusual window and built-in cabinets. The dining room is to the right, just a short trip from the kitchen. Here, the family chef will appreciate a work island/snack bar combination, a walk-in pantry and a corner window sink. A bayed nook offers access to a screened porch—two great spots for casual meals or afternoon tea. There's also a covered porch off the great room, which has an impressive fireplace flanked by cabinets.

First Floor: 2,172 square feet
Second Floor: 690 square feet
Total: 2,862 square feet

Bonus Space: 450 square feet
Width: 72'-0" Depth: 73'-0"

DESIGN HPT880042

Spacious Gathering Room

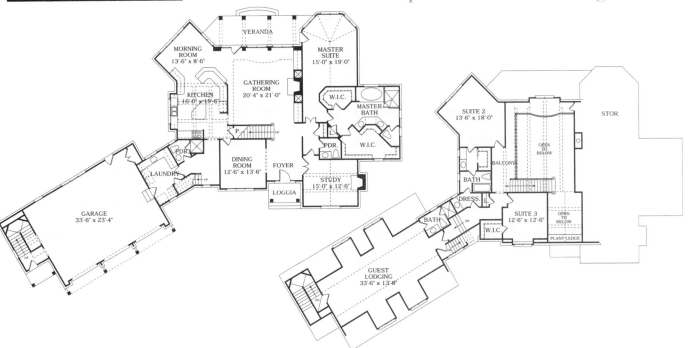

Gently curved arches and dormers contrast with the straight lines of gables and wooden columns on this French-style stone exterior. Small-paned windows are enhanced by shutters; tall chimneys and a cupola add height. Inside, a spacious gathering room with an impressive fireplace opens to a cheery morning room. The kitchen is a delight, with a beam ceiling, triangular work island, walk-in pantry and angular counter with a snack bar. The nearby laundry room includes a sink, a work area and plenty of room for storage. The first-floor master suite boasts a bay-windowed sitting nook, a deluxe bath and a handy study.

First Floor: 2,660 square feet
Second Floor: 914 square feet
Total: 3,574 square feet

Bonus Space: 733 square feet
Width: 114'-8" Depth: 75'-10"

Bayed Sitting Area

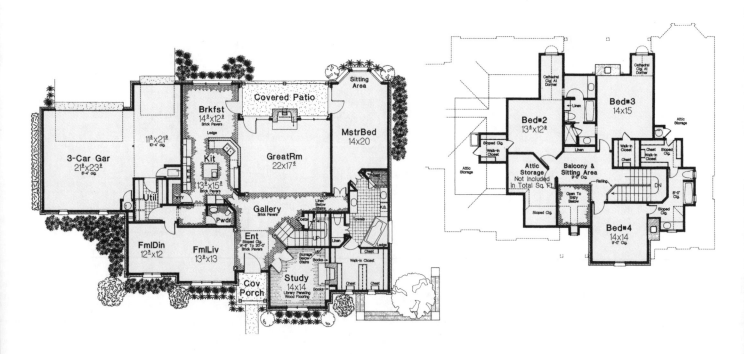

Stones with brick accents create an exterior with real country charm. The feeling continues inside, where brick pavers are used as flooring for the entry, gallery, kitchen and breakfast room. To the left of the entry, the formal living and dining rooms range across the front of the house, while a study with wood flooring, bookshelves and a fireplace is to the right. The great room also boasts a fireplace, as well as access to a covered patio. The master suite includes a bayed sitting area, walk-in closets and an elegant bath with dual vanities and an angled garden tub. Upstairs, two bedrooms share a bath that includes twin vanities, while a third bedroom has a private bath. A sitting area in the balcony overlooks the entry.

First Floor: 2,612 square feet
Second Floor: 1,242 square feet
Total: 3,854 square feet

Width: 84'-0" Depth: 55'-7"

DESIGN HPT880044

A taste of Europe is reflected in arched windows topped off by keystones in this traditional design. Formal rooms flank the foyer, which leads to a two-story family room with a focal-point fireplace. The sunny breakfast nook opens to a private covered porch through a French door. A spacious, well-organized kitchen features angled, wrapping counters, double ovens and a walk-in pantry. The garage offers a service entrance to the utility area and pantry. An angled staircase leads from the two-story foyer to sleeping quarters upstairs. Here, a gallery hall with a balcony overlooks the foyer and family room and connects family bedrooms. A private hall leads to the master suite. It boasts a well-lit sitting area, a walk-in closet with linen storage and a lavish bath with a vaulted ceiling and plant shelves. Please specify basement or crawlspace foundation when ordering.

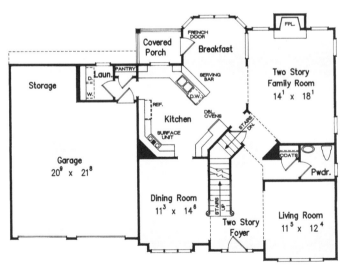

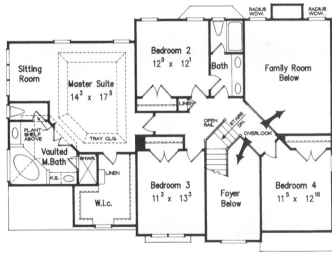

First Floor: 1,205 square feet
Second Floor: 1,277 square feet
Total: 2,482 square feet

Width: 53'-6" Depth: 39'-4"

Built-In China Cabinet

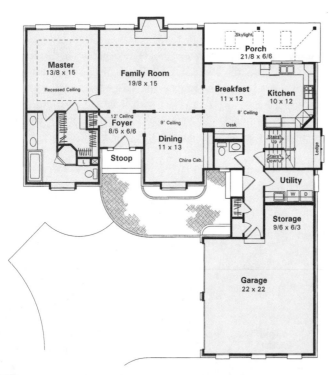

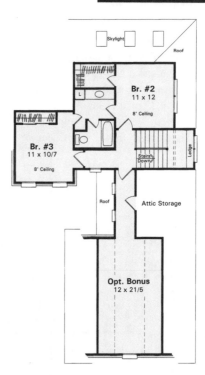

The multi-level hipped rooflines and right-angle garage create a cozy sense of enclosure in this spacious two-story home. The first floor is centered around an enormous family room, just past the foyer, with a fireplace flanked by windows in the rear wall. The master suite comprises the left side of the plan with a recessed ceiling in the bedroom and an L-shaped bath with dual lavatory and separate shower and tub. To the right of the plan, the large U-shaped kitchen is open to the breakfast area, which offers a built-in desk and sliding doors to the skylit covered porch. The formal dining room with a nine-foot ceiling features a built-in china cabinet. Two additional bedrooms upstairs adjoin a shared bath with a separate tub and toilet compartment.

First Floor: 1,520 square feet
Second Floor: 489 square feet
Total: 2,009 square feet

Width: 57'-0" Depth: 61'-6"

DESIGN HPT880046

Spacious Breakfast Room

AEuropean feel is shown on the exterior facade of this exciting two-story home and hints at the exquisite grace of the interior. The sensational view at the foyer includes high windows across the rear wall, a fireplace, open stairs with rich wood trim and volume ceilings. The formal dining room offers dimension to the entry and is conveniently located for serving from the kitchen. The spacious breakfast room, wraparound bar

in the kitchen and open hearth room offer a cozy gathering place for family members. The deluxe master bedroom boasts an eleven-foot ceiling, a sitting area and a garden bath. The second-floor balcony leads to a bedroom suite with a private bath and two additional bedrooms with large closets and private access to a shared bath.

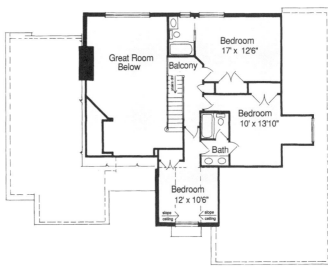

First Floor: 1,915 square feet
Second Floor: 823 square feet
Total: 2,738 square feet

Width: 63'-4" Depth: 48'-0"

Gently Curved Arches

DESIGN HPT880047

This stucco home contrasts gently curved arches with gables and uses large multi-pane windows to flood the interior with natural light. Square pillars form an impressive entry, leading to a two-story foyer. The living room is set apart from the informal area of the house and could serve as a cozy study instead. The back patio can be reached from both the breakfast nook and the family room, which features a cathedral ceiling and a fireplace. The master suite offers two walk-in closets and a bath with twin vanities, a garden tub and separate shower.

First Floor: 1,904 square feet
Second Floor: 645 square feet
Total: 2,549 square feet

Bonus Room: 434 square feet
Width: 71'-2" Depth: 45'-8"

DESIGN HPT880048

Impressive Entrance

An impressive two-story entrance welcomes you to this state-ly home. Massive chimneys and pillars and varying rooflines add interest to the stucco exterior. The foyer, lighted by a clerestory window, opens to the formal living and dining rooms. The living room—which could also serve as a study—features a fireplace, as does the family room. Both rooms access the patio.

The L-shaped island kitchen opens to a bay-windowed breakfast nook, which is echoed by the sitting area in the master suite. A room next to the kitchen could serve as a bedroom or a home office. The second floor contains two family bedrooms plus a bonus room for future expansion.

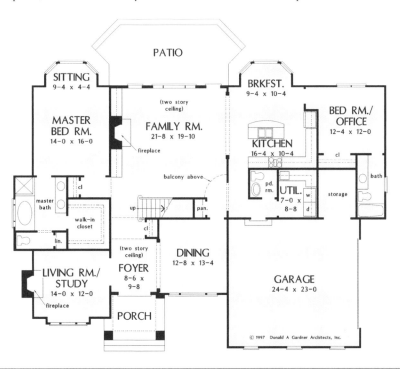

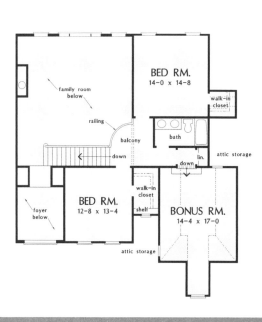

First Floor: 2,249 square feet
Second Floor: 620 square feet
Total: 2,869 square feet

Bonus Room: 308 square feet
Width: 69'-6" Depth: 52'-0"

Rambling Master Suite

This European-style home offers an array of stunning windows that serve both aesthetic and practical purposes. Inside, the foyer leads to the grand staircase and balcony overlook above. A food-prep island defines the space between the breakfast area and the kitchen. The kitchen also contains dual ovens, extra counter space and a sizable pantry. The rambling master suite features a sitting room, fireplace, full bath and two walk-in closets. Please specify basement or slab foundation when ordering.

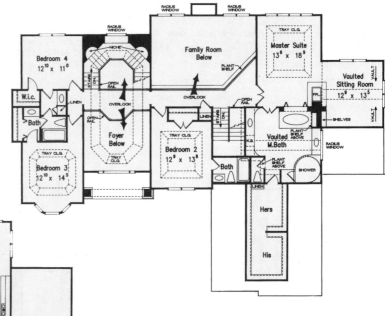

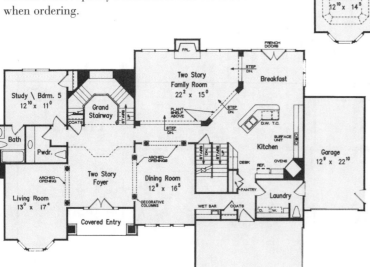

First Floor: 2,190 square feet
Second Floor: 1,865 square feet
Total: 4,055 square feet

Width: 79'-0" Depth: 60'-4"

DESIGN HPT880050

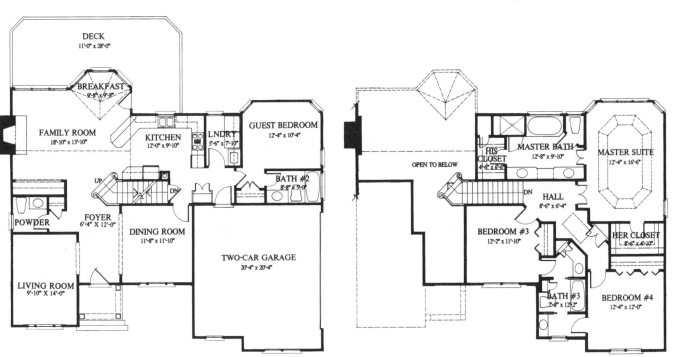

DECK
11'-0" x 28'-0"

BREAKFAST
9'-8" x 9'-8"

FAMILY ROOM
18'-10" x 13'-10"

KITCHEN
12'-0" x 9'-10"

LNDRY
5'-6" x 7'-10"

GUEST BEDROOM
12'-4" x 10'-4"

BATH #2
8'-8" x 5'-0"

POWDER

FOYER
6'-4" X 12'-0"

DINING ROOM
11'-8" x 11'-10"

TWO-CAR GARAGE
20'-4" x 20'-4"

LIVING ROOM
9'-10" X 14'-0"

OPEN TO BELOW

HIS CLOSET
4'-6" x 6'-5"

MASTER BATH
12'-8" x 9'-10"

MASTER SUITE
12'-4" x 16'-6"

HALL
8'-6" x 6'-4"

BEDROOM #3
12'-2" x 11'-10"

HER CLOSET
8'-6" x 4'-10"

BATH #3
7'-8" x 12'-2"

BEDROOM #4
12'-4" x 12'-0"

This elegant European-style house easily accommodates formal entertaining, with a foyer that opens to a living room on the left and a dining room on the right. Introduce your guests to the warmth of the family room with its cozy fireplace and expansive views. The first floor also makes room for a guest bedroom and a full bath. The second floor holds three additional bedrooms. The master suite, with His and Hers closets, is sure to delight. This home is designed with a walkout basement foundation.

First Floor: 1,270 square feet
Second Floor: 1,070 square feet
Total: 2,340 square feet

Width: 50'-0" Depth: 44'-0"

Study with Beam Ceiling

Unusual chimneys, varied rooflines and European window treatments enhance the stone-and-stucco exterior of this breathtaking home. A petite portico welcomes you into the two-story foyer. Inside, the heart of the home is the great room, featuring a fireplace flanked by bookcases, a snack bar and two doors to the rear terrace. A semi-circle of windows outlines the breakfast nook, which opens off the kitchen, a wonderful work area with a cooktop island, a walk-in pantry and ample counter space. The formal dining room is a few steps from both the kitchen and the front door, making entertaining easy. To the left of the foyer, a study with a beam ceiling and a second fireplace serves as a quiet retreat.

First Floor: 2,145 square feet
Second Floor: 1,310 square feet
Total: 3,455 square feet

Bonus Space: 308 square feet
Width: 67'-0" Depth: 59'-4"

DESIGN HPT880052

Guest Apartment

Multi-pane windows complement the porte cochere and dress up the natural stone facade of this French country estate. A two-story foyer leads to a central grand room with French doors to the terrace. A formal dining room to the front offers a fireplace. To the left, a cozy study with a second fireplace features built-in cabinetry and is close to a convenient powder room. The sleeping quarters offer luxurious amenities. Upstairs, three suites, each with a walk-in closet and one with its own bath, share a balcony hall that leads to a home theater. A guest apartment over the garage will house visiting or live-in relatives, or may be used as a maid's quarters.

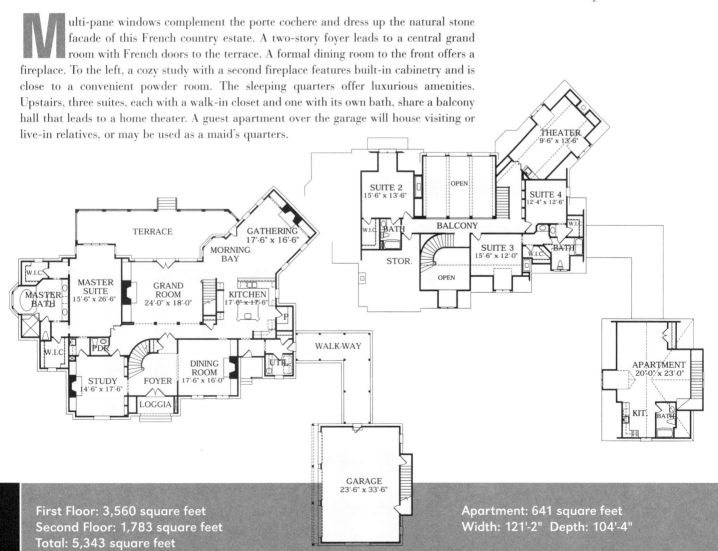

First Floor: 3,560 square feet
Second Floor: 1,783 square feet
Total: 5,343 square feet

Apartment: 641 square feet
Width: 121'-2" **Depth:** 104'-4"

Columns and Arches

A garage with barn doors and unusual shingled dormers gives this French country home a true country look. Stone accents and wooden shutters add to the appeal. A recessed entry opens to the foyer, where columns and arches define the dining and living rooms. A butler's pantry leads to the island kitchen, part of a large open area that includes a sizable nook and a vaulted family room. Notice the built-ins, the through-fireplace and the wall of windows across the back of the house. To the right of the foyer are a den and the master suite, which offers a large walk-in closet and a fine bath.

First Floor: 2,532 square feet
Second Floor: 650 square feet
Total: 3,182 square feet

Bonus Space: 383 square feet
Width: 80'-0" Depth: 77'-6"

French Country Charm

A stone-and-stucco exterior and exquisite window detailing give this home its Mediterranean appeal. A covered porch connects the garage to the main house via the breakfast room. The master suite includes two walk-in closets and a bath with separate vanities. Two family bedrooms in the lower level feature walk-in closets and share a compartmented bath and a media/recreation room. Both bedrooms offer private access to the patio. A utility room and storage room complete this level.

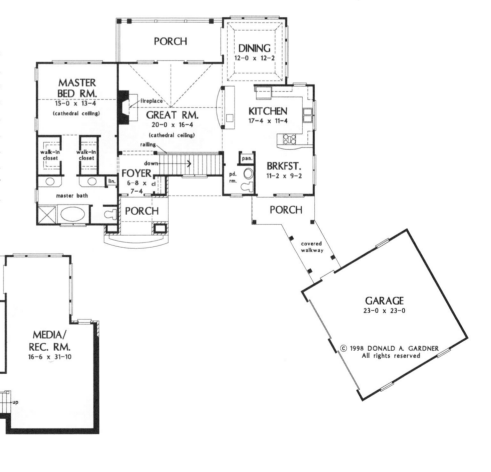

PORCH

DINING
12-0 x 12-2

MASTER
BED RM.
15-0 x 13-4
(cathedral ceiling)

fireplace

KITCHEN
17-4 x 11-4

GREAT RM.
20-0 x 16-4
(cathedral ceiling)

railing

walk-in closet

walk-in closet

down

pan.

BRKFST.
11-2 x 9-2

FOYER
6-8 x cl
7-4

lin.

pd. rm.

master bath

PORCH

PORCH

covered walkway

GARAGE
23-0 x 23-0

© 1998 DONALD A. GARDNER
All rights reserved

PATIO

COVERED PATIO

BED RM.
11-6 x 13-0

bath

lin.

BED RM.
12-0 x 13-0

MEDIA/
REC. RM.
16-6 x 31-10

walk-in closet

walk-in closet

STORAGE
(unfinished)

UTIL.
8-10 x
6-10

d   w

up

Main Level: 1,472 square feet
Lower Level: 1,211 square feet
Total: 2,683 square feet

Width: 54'-0" Depth: 40'-8"

Dramatic Ceiling Treatments

DESIGN HPT880055

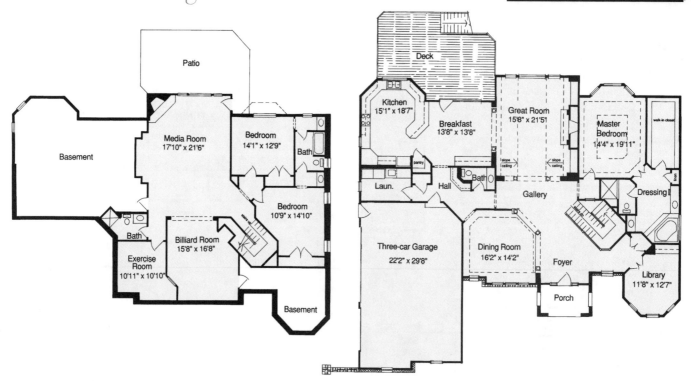

Stone accents provide warmth and character to the exterior of this home. An arched entry leads to the interior, where elegant window styles and dramatic ceiling treatments create an impressive showplace. The gourmet kitchen and breakfast room offer a spacious area for chores and family gatherings, while providing a striking view through the great room to the fireplace. An extravagant master suite and a library with built-in shelves round out the main level. On the lower level, two additional bedrooms, a media room, a billiards room and an exercise room complete the home.

Main Level: 2,582 square feet
Lower Level: 1,746 square feet
Total: 4,328 square feet

Width: 70'-8" Depth: 64'-0"

DESIGN HPT880056

This French-style home is designed for a sloping lot, with the garage at the basement level. The stone-and-stucco exterior is highlighted by interesting windows, corner quoins and a variety of gables. Inside, the two-story foyer is flanked by the formal living and dining rooms, both of which are lighted by bay windows. The family room features a fireplace and access to the sun deck. An efficient kitchen opens to a glass-walled breakfast room and provides a snack bar that serves the entire informal living area. Completing the first floor, the master bedroom includes a compartmented bath with a walk-in closet and twin vanities. Upstairs, three family bedrooms share a good-sized bath and views of much of the first floor.

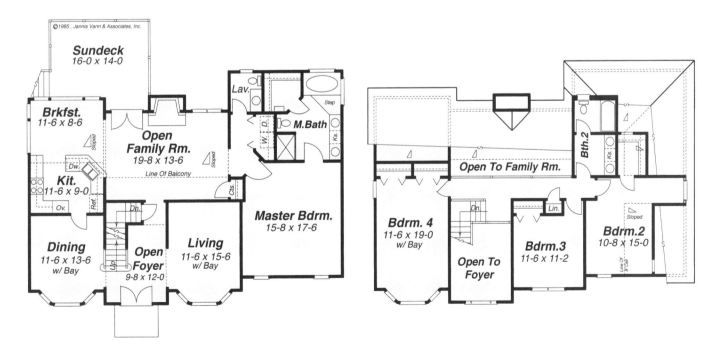

First Floor: 1,560 square feet
Second Floor: 834 square feet
Total: 2,394 square feet

Width: 50'-0" Depth: 47'-0"

Splendid Family Room

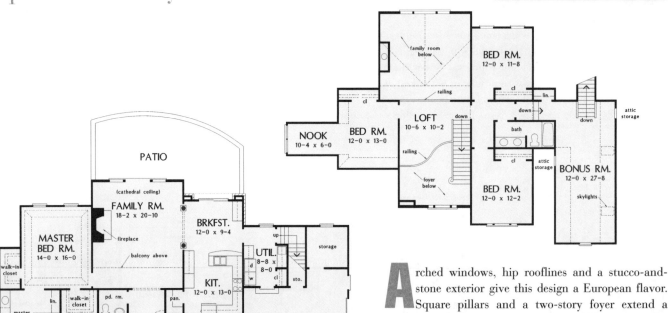

Arched windows, hip rooflines and a stucco-and-stone exterior give this design a European flavor. Square pillars and a two-story foyer extend a warm welcome to a floor plan designed for convenience. The formal dining room opens from the foyer and is easily served by the U-shaped kitchen. A breakfast nook offers a pleasant place for casual meals or coffee with friends. The family room will be the heart of the home, with a cathedral ceiling, a fireplace and access to the patio. If you choose to make the front-facing living room a study instead, the family room works well for formal as well as informal gatherings. ©1997 Donald A. Gardner Architects, Inc.

First Floor: 1,904 square feet
Second Floor: 903 square feet
Total: 2,807 square feet

Bonus Room: 434 square feet
Width: 71'-2" Depth: 45'-8"

DESIGN HPT880058

Commanding Presence

A lovely double arch gives this European-style home a commanding presence. Once inside, a two-story foyer provides an open view directly through the formal living room to the rear grounds beyond. The spacious kitchen with a work island and the bayed breakfast area share space with the family room. The private master suite features dual sinks, twin walk-in closets, a corner garden tub and a separate shower. A large game room completes this wonderful family home. Please specify basement, crawlspace or slab foundation when ordering.

Cost to build? See page 214 to order complete cost estimate to build this house in your area!

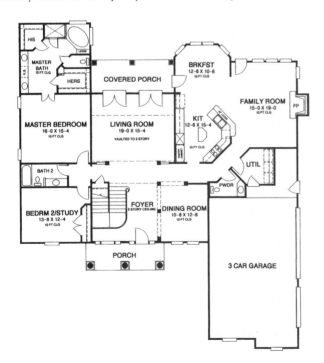

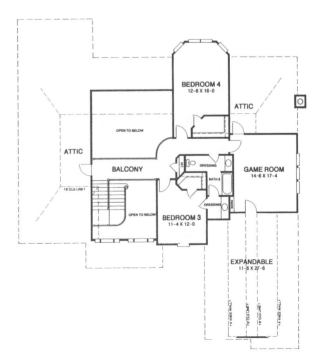

First Floor: 2,469 square feet
Second Floor: 1,025 square feet
Total: 3,494 square feet

Bonus Space: 320 square feet
Width: 67'-8" Depth: 74'-2"

L

Impressive French Facade

DESIGN HPT880059

Arches and gables contrast and complement in a recurring theme on this impressive French exterior. Note particularly the clerestory window over the foyer. Formal living and dining rooms open off the foyer, providing a large area for entertaining. A sun deck expands outdoor living possibilities, with access from the breakfast room and the family room. A fireplace in the family room spreads cheer throughout the informal area. To the left of the plan, the master wing includes a deluxe bath, two walk-in closets and a sitting room with access to a privacy deck. The second floor offers three bedrooms, two baths and a bonus room for future use.

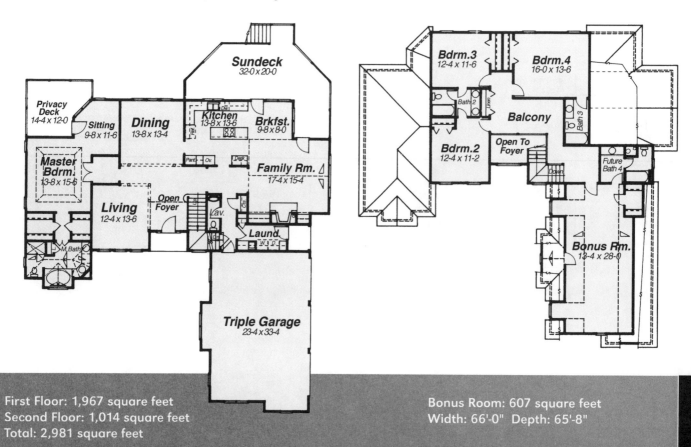

First Floor: 1,967 square feet
Second Floor: 1,014 square feet
Total: 2,981 square feet

Bonus Room: 607 square feet
Width: 66'-0" Depth: 65'-8"

DESIGN HPT880060

Captain's Quarters

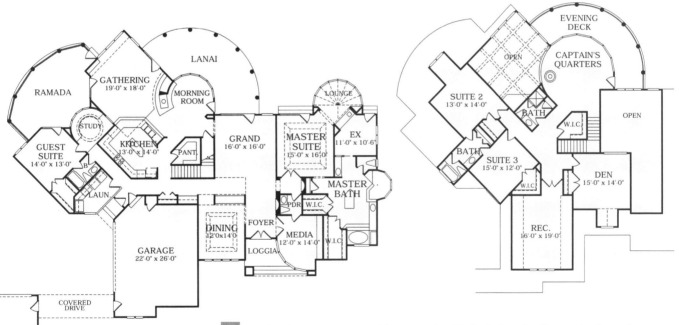

From the elegant entrance with a curved wall of windows leading to the front door, to the wonderful angles used throughout the home, this is a plan sure to please. Study the master suite and you'll see that amenities haven't been neglected: two walk-in closets, a lavish bath with a separate tub and shower and two vanities, a separate unique lounge and an exercise room. On the other end of the home, find the highly efficient kitchen, a spacious gathering room, a round morning room and study, and a quiet guest suite. The second level is equally deluxe with two suites, a recreation room, a quiet den and a large open area called the captain's quarters that opens out to an evening deck.

First Floor: 3,329 square feet
Second Floor: 1,485 square feet
Total: 4,814 square feet

Bonus Space: 300 square feet
Width: 106'-6" Depth: 89'-10"

Vaulted Bath with Garden Tub

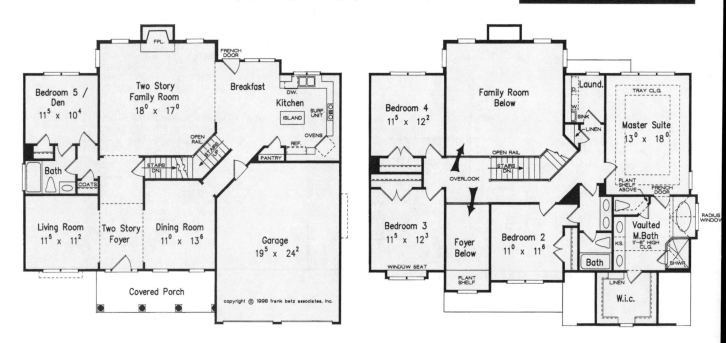

Siding and shutters add a charming country style to this traditional home. The family room is flanked by the kitchen/breakfast area and a bedroom that doubles as a den. Upstairs, four bedrooms overlook the family room and foyer. Bedroom 3 features a window seat. Adorned with a tray ceiling and a ribbon of windows, the master suite enjoys many amenities including a plant shelf, vaulted bath, garden tub set in a box-bay window, separate shower and walk-in closet. A second-floor laundry ensures that wash day will be a breeze. Please specify basement, crawlspace or slab foundation when ordering.

First Floor: 1,306 square feet
Second Floor: 1,276 square feet
Total: 2,582 square feet

Width: 50'-0" Depth: 45'-4"

DESIGN HPT880062

Secluded Master Lounge

A gently sloping, high-pitched roof complements keystones, arch-top windows and a delicate balcony balustrade, and calls up a sense of cozy elegance. The foyer opens to a grand room with a focal-point fireplace and access to a screened room that leads to the veranda. The gourmet kitchen offers a walk-in pantry, acres of counter space and a morning room with outdoor flow. An island wardrobe highlights the master suite, which boasts a secluded lounge with a door to a private area of the veranda. Upstairs, two secondary bedrooms enjoy a balcony overlook to the foyer, and each room has its own access to an outdoor deck.

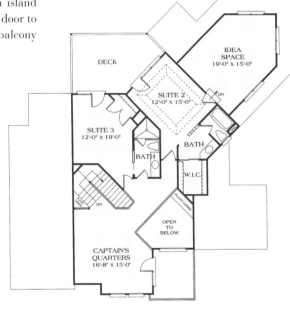

First Floor: 1,862 square feet
Second Floor: 1,044 square feet
Total: 2,906 square feet

Width: 60'-0" Depth: 60'-0"

© American Home Gallery, Ltd.

Covered Veranda

Dual chimneys (one a false chimney created to enhance the aesthetic effect) and a double stairway to the covered entry of this home create a balanced architectural statement. The sunlit foyer leads straight into the spacious great room, where French doors provide a generous view of the covered veranda in back. The great room features a tray ceiling and a fireplace, bordered by twin bookcases. Another great view is offered from the spacious kitchen with a breakfast bar and a roomy work island. The master suite provides a large balanced bath and a spacious closet. This home is designed with a walkout basement foundation.

QUOTE ONE®

Cost to build? See page 214 to order complete cost estimate to build this house in your area!

2-CAR GARAGE
21'-6" X 21'-0"

LAUNDRY   STORAGE   VERANDA

MASTER BATH

BREAKFAST
13'-6" X 10'-0"

MASTER SUITE
15'-9" X 16'-0"

W.I.C.

UP

GREAT ROOM
20'-6" x 17'-6"

KITCHEN
16'-0" X 13'-6"

DN.

BEDROOM NO. 3
12'-0" X 13'-3"

POWDER

PANTRY

DINING ROOM
13'-3" X 14'-9"

FOYER

BEDROOM NO. 2
12'-6" X 13'-3"

BATH

PORTICO

Square Footage: 2,697

Width: 65'-3" **Depth:** 67'-3"

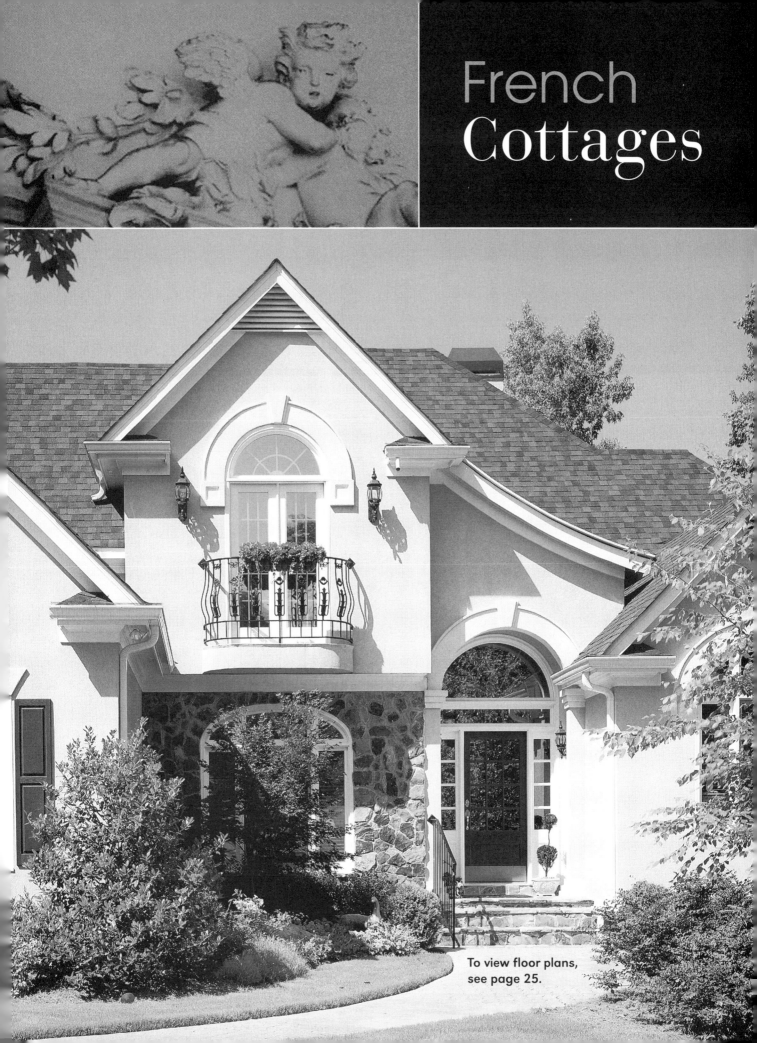

French
Cottages

To view floor plans, see page 25.

Side Courtyard

family
21-6 x 17

mbr
13-4 x 16

dining
15 x 13-4

m bath

brkfst

18 x 16

kit

br 2
13-4 x 12

foyer

laundry

porch

garage
20-1 x 18

br 3
11 x 13

Presenting a narrow frontage, this plan extends back 75 feet and provides spacious rooms for a family. Enter the home through a front corner porch or through a side courtyard that opens to the dining room. A fireplace warms the family room, which accesses the rear yard through French doors. A bright corner breakfast nook highlights the kitchen, which provides a cooktop island and laundry-room access. The master suite features a walk-in closet and separate vanities in the compartmented bath. Each of two secondary bedrooms provides a walk-in closet.

Square Footage: 2,048

Width: 38'-10" Depth: 75'-0"

DESIGN HPT880065

Spacious Living Room

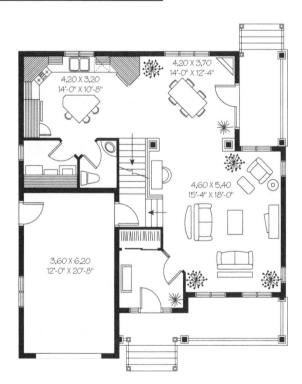

4,20 X 3,20
14'-0" X 10'-8"

4,20 X 3,70
14'-0" X 12'-4"

4,60 X 5,40
15'-4" X 18'-0"

3,60 X 6,20
12'-0" X 20'-8"

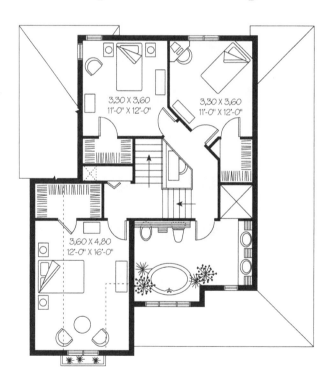

3,30 X 3,60
11'-0" X 12'-0"

3,30 X 3,60
11'-0" X 12'-0"

3,60 X 4,80
12'-0" X 16'-0"

A flower box, covered front porch and horizontal siding combine to give this home plenty of appeal. Inside, the foyer is designed as an air lock, preventing cold air from disturbing the family. An open living area provides a spacious feeling, with the dining area defined by columns. The corner kitchen features an island snack bar, a window sink and tons of cabinet and counter space. Note the covered porch just off the dining area—perfect for dining alfresco. Upstairs, three bedrooms—each with a walk-in closet—share a lavish bath. This home is deisgned with a basement foundation.

First Floor: 896 square feet
Second Floor: 948 square feet
Total: 1,844 square feet

Width: 35'-4" Depth: 39'-8"

Provençal Accents

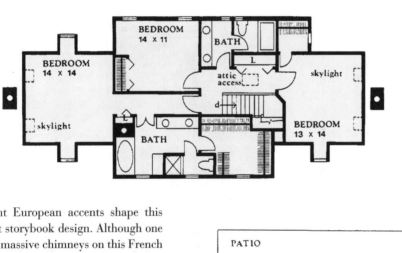

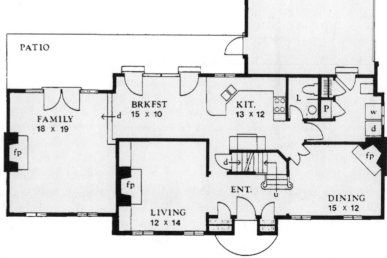

Eloquent European accents shape this quaint storybook design. Although one of the massive chimneys on this French stucco home is decorative, fireplaces in the family, living and dining rooms will ensure that you have no trouble keeping warm. The front of the house appears symmetrical, but the front door is off-center, adding a bit of eccentricity. The entrance opens into the formal rooms, then leads back to the kitchen, which opens into a breakfast area with French doors to the patio. The sunken family room also accesses the patio. A garage and laundry room complete the first floor. Upstairs, skylights brighten the interior of two of the three bedrooms.

First Floor: 1,407 square feet
Second Floor: 1,157 square feet
Total: 2,564 square feet

Width: 62'-3" Depth: 51'-2"

Delightful Arbor

Architectural elements borrowed from English Tudor style combine with French country details to make this eclectic creation a picture-perfect European cottage. The exterior is enhanced with steeply pitched rooflines, multi-pane windows and a private front terrace complete with a delightful arbor. The entry contains a wood-railing staircase and opens to the formal bow-windowed dining room. To the right, a galley kitchen and its adjacent breakfast area lead to a private terrace. The great room features a partially vaulted ceiling and a fireplace flanked by built-in bookshelves. The master suite enjoys a relaxing master bath and twin walk-in closets.

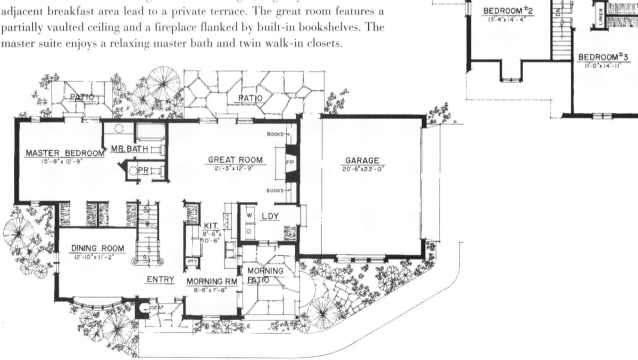

First Floor: 1,182 square feet
Second Floor: 716 square feet
Total: 1,898 square feet

Width: 68'-5" Depth: 33'-5"

French Countryside

DESIGN HPT880069

4,20 X 3,20
14'-0" X 10'-8"

3,60 X 3,70
12'-0" X 12'-4"

3,60 X 4,80
12'-0" X 16'-0"

3,90 X 3,70
13'-0" X 12'-4"

2,80 X 3,70
9'-4" X 12'-4"

3,60 X 3,60
12'-0" X 12'-0"

This small stucco home would go equally well in the French countryside or in your new neighborhood. A covered front entrance leads straight ahead to the kitchen, where an interesting angled counter is flanked by a writing desk and a pantry. A snack bar separates the kitchen from the family room, which receives natural light from large windows and sliding glass doors to the rear covered porch. Everyone will appreciate the fireplace in the living room and the pocket door between the kitchen and the dining room. This home is designed with a basement foundation.

First Floor: 957 square feet
Second Floor: 885 square feet
Total: 1,842 square feet

Width: 38'-0" Depth: 30'-0"

DESIGN HPT880070

Here's a comfortable cottage with plenty of windows to bring in views and fresh air. An open interior allows flexible space and room for family and friends to gather. A gourmet kitchen provides a food preparation counter and an inviting breakfast area that leads out to the rear covered porch. Triple-window views in the family room take advantage of the gorgeous scenery, while a fireplace and an entertainment center warm up the interior atmosphere. A private vestibule leads to the master suite, which boasts a walk-in closet and a dual vanity. Upstairs, two secondary bedrooms share a computer loft.

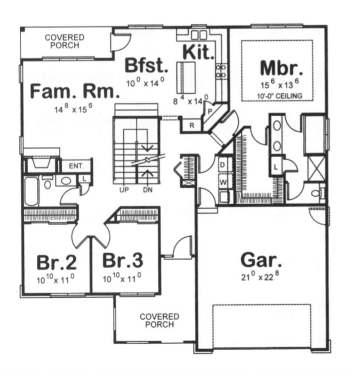

First Floor: 1,724 square feet
Second Floor: 701 square feet
Total: 2,425 square feet

Width: 50'-0" Depth: 51'-8"

Plenty of Curb Appeal

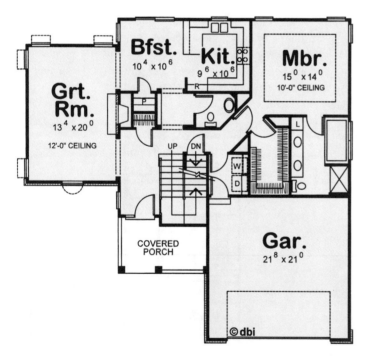

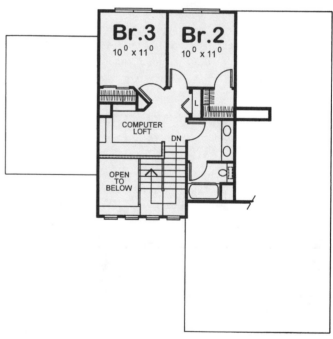

Stucco and stone combine with shutters and multi-pane windows, giving this three-bedroom home plenty of curb appeal. A covered front porch leads to the two-story foyer, where an elegant staircase offsets an archway that leads to the great room. This room offers a warming fireplace, a twelve foot ceiling and plenty of windows. The C-shaped kitchen is both con-venient and sweet, with a window sink and adjacent breakfast room. The first-floor master suite is sure to please with a ten-foot ceiling, large walk-in closet and a pampering bath. Upstairs, two family bedrooms share a full bath that includes dual vanities, and a computer loft with built-ins.

First Floor: 1,302 square feet
Second Floor: 516 square feet
Total: 1,818 square feet

Width: 50'-0" Depth: 48'-0"

DESIGN HPT880072

Bayed Breakfast Nook

A covered stoop topped by a standing-seam roof provides an elegant entry for this charming European-style cottage, where shuttered windows complement the stucco exterior. Inside, columns define the dining room, which sits to the right of the entry; to the left, a cozy living room can double as a study. The family room, warmed by a fireplace, adjoins a bayed breakfast nook. The nearby island kitchen serves formal and informal gatherings with ease. Upstairs, three family bedrooms, one with a private bath, join the luxurious master suite. Here, a private sitting area boasts a second fireplace and the lavish bath features a dual-vanity sink, whirlpool tub and walk-in closet.

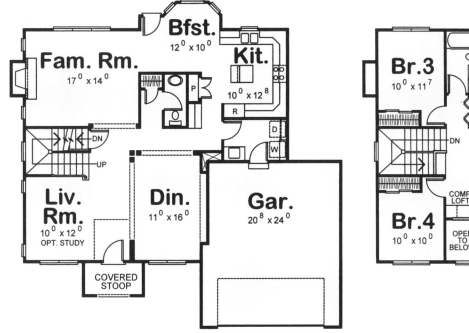

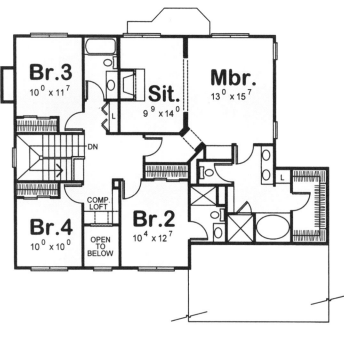

First Floor: 1,234 square feet
Second Floor: 1,316 square feet
Total: 2,550 square feet

Width: 48'-0" Depth: 48'-0"

Computer Loft

Here's a sumptuous retreat with plenty of space for family members as well as guests—introduced by a very charming facade. At the heart of the home, a spacious great room boasts a fireplace framed by tall windows that allow great views. Decorative columns define an open arrangement of the foyer, living area and breakfast nook. A charming window seat resides in the stairwell's landing. Second-floor sleeping quarters include three secondary bedrooms, one of which is a suite with a shower bath. The upper hall leads to an overlook of the foyer and offers a computer loft with built-in shelves.

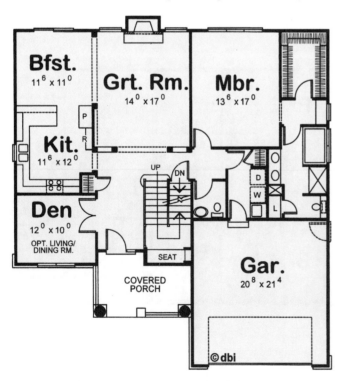

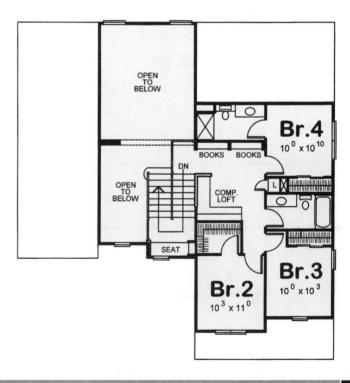

First Floor: 1,538 square feet
Second Floor: 727 square feet
Total: 2,265 square feet

Width: 48'-4" Depth: 50'-0"

DESIGN HPT880074

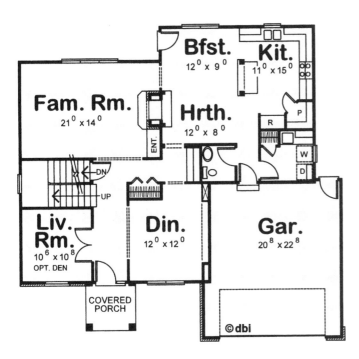

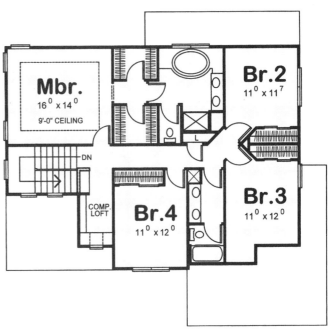

Matchstick trim and shutters provide rich embellishments and add a Tudor flavor to this European facade. A thoroughly modern interior begins with a gallery foyer that opens to a formal dining room and a flex room that converts to a den. The spacious family room provides a built-in entertainment center and shares a through-fireplace with a hearth room. A gourmet kitchen features a food-preparation island, a walk-in pantry and wrapping counters. Upstairs, the master suite offers a dressing area framed by walk-in closets. Three secondary bedrooms are connected by a hall that provides additional linen storage.

First Floor: 1,369 square feet
Second Floor: 1,239 square feet
Total: 2,608 square feet

Width: 49'-0" Depth: 46'-4"

Accented by Arches

This stunning design is dazzled in stucco and stone accents. A giant front window illuminates the formal dining room accented by arches. The foyer welcomes you into the vaulted great room, warmed by an enormous hearth. The kitchen is set between the dining and breakfast rooms for convenience. The master wing provides a vaulted master bath and huge walk-in closet. On the opposite side of the home, three additional family bedrooms share a hall bath. A handy laundry room completes the floor plan.

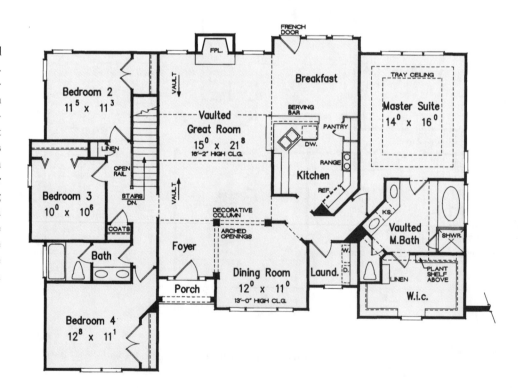

Square Footage: 2,032

Width: 58'-6" Depth: 43'-10"

DESIGN HPT880076

Varied rooflines, keystones and arches set off a stucco exterior that's highlighted by a stone turret and a bay with three divided-light windows. Inside, the master suite enjoys a tray ceiling and floor-to-ceiling light from a sitting room. The formal dining room leads to a private covered porch for after-dinner conversation on pleasant evenings. The central kitchen boasts a built-in planning desk, an ample pantry and an angled counter that overlooks the breakfast room. Sleeping quarters include a first-floor master suite with a vaulted bath and a plant shelf, and two second-floor family bedrooms that share a balcony overlook and a full bath. Please specify basement, crawlspace or slab foundation when ordering.

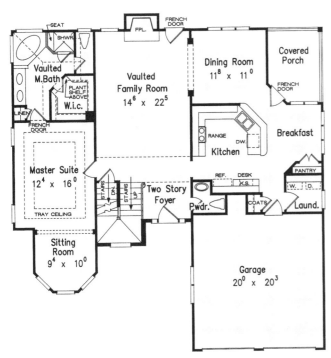

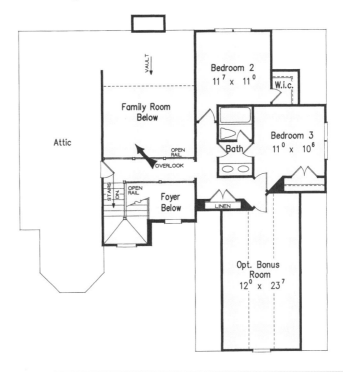

First Floor: 1,398 square feet
Second Floor: 515 square feet
Total: 1,913 square feet

Bonus Room: 282 square feet
Width: 48'-0" Depth: 50'-10"

Fieldstone Hearth

Arched window highlights detail the ornate stone and stucco exterior of this two-story French modern design. A stepped, covered entry with a guest closet leads directly to the family room, which offers a sloped ceiling and a fireplace with a fieldstone hearth. The master suite features a vaulted ceiling, a full bath and lots of closet space. The area containing the large corner kitchen and breakfast area offers a built-in desk and pantry. Lying just beyond this area are a powder room, utility room and entrance to the two-car garage. Three additional bedrooms featuring generous closets are upstairs.

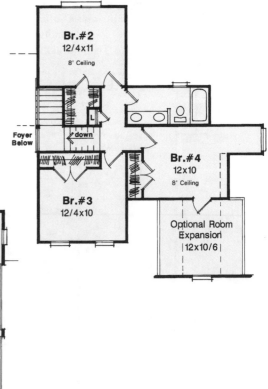

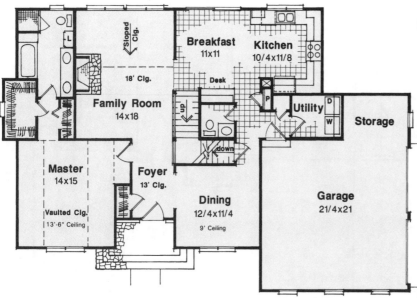

First Floor: 1,395 square feet
Second Floor: 629 square feet
Total: 2,024 square feet

Width: 60'-0" Depth: 40'-0"

DESIGN HPT880078

Luxurious Livability

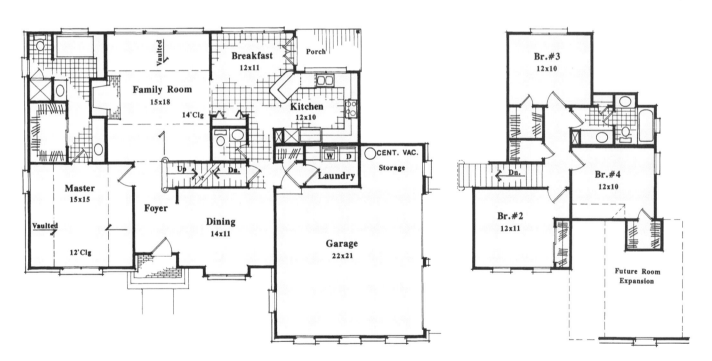

T he hipped roof is aligned with gables on the sides, while a third gable is centered on the roofline. Inside, vaulted ceilings and a comfortable floor plan complete the feeling of luxurious livability. The master suite features a twelve-foot vaulted ceiling. The private bath is nearly as large as the master bedroom and includes a walk-in closet, garden tub and separate shower. The family room is accented by a fourteen-foot vaulted ceiling, a brick fireplace and a wall of windows. The U-shaped kitchen provides an angled island and is open to the breakfast room, which accesses the porch through double doors. The formal dining room offers a full-height bay window and is comfortably isolated from the kitchen.

First Floor: 1,441 square feet
Second Floor: 632 square feet
Total: 2,073 square feet

Bonus Space: 150 square feet
Width: 58'-0" Depth: 44'-0"

Elegant Ceiling Details

Arched openings, decorative columns and elegant ceiling details throughout highlight this livable floor plan. The country kitchen includes a spacious work area, preparation island, serving bar to the great room and breakfast nook with a tray ceiling. Set to the rear for gracious entertaining, the dining room opens to the great room. Note the warming fireplace and French-door access to the backyard in the great room. The master suite is beautifully appointed with a tray ceiling, bay window, compartmented bath and walk-in closet. Two family bedrooms sharing a full bath, laundry room and powder room complete this gracious design. Please specify basement, crawlspace or slab foundation when ordering.

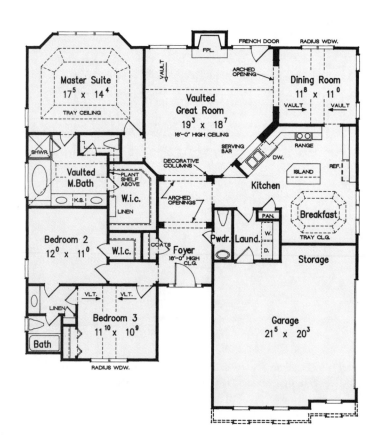

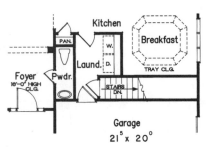

Optional Basement Stair Location

Square Footage: 1,884

Width: 50'-0" Depth: 55'-4"

94

DESIGN HPT880080

Optional Bonus Room

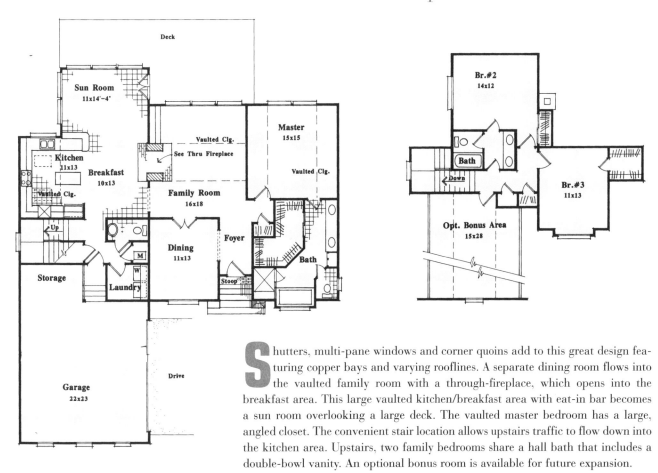

Shutters, multi-pane windows and corner quoins add to this great design featuring copper bays and varying rooflines. A separate dining room flows into the vaulted family room with a through-fireplace, which opens into the breakfast area. This large vaulted kitchen/breakfast area with eat-in bar becomes a sun room overlooking a large deck. The vaulted master bedroom has a large, angled closet. The convenient stair location allows upstairs traffic to flow down into the kitchen area. Upstairs, two family bedrooms share a hall bath that includes a double-bowl vanity. An optional bonus room is available for future expansion.

First Floor: 1,670 square feet
Second Floor: 540 square feet
Total: 2,210 square feet

Bonus Space: 455 square feet
Width: 54'-0" Depth: 61'-0"

Cathedral Ceiling

First Floor:

PATIO

GREAT RM.
16-2 x 21-2
(cathedral ceiling)
fireplace

MASTER BED RM.
13-0 x 14-4

BRKFST.
11-4 x 9-10

UTIL.
8-0 x
8-11

storage

balcony above

walk-in closet

KIT.
11-4 x 11-6

lin.

cl

pd. rm.

master bath

cl

up

FOYER
10-6 x 6-11

DINING
11-4 x 12-10

GARAGE
21-0 x 23-8

PORCH

© 1996 Donald A. Gardner Architects, Inc.

Second Floor:

great room below

BED RM.
11-4 x 13-8

railing

cl

attic storage

attic storage

down

down

cl

attic storage

skylights

lin.

bath

BONUS RM.
12-0 x 27-4

foyer below

BED RM.
11-4 x 13-10

The interplay of gables and rooflines results in an appealing exterior, further enhanced by arched windows, shutters and sturdy columns. Upon entering, guests will look into the great room and through to the patio, a perfect spot for sampling hors d'oeuvres, weather permitting. The fireplace in the great room will be welcome when it's chilly outside. The kitchen is found midway between the formal dining room and the breakfast nook, and offers a snack bar for quick meals. The master suite fills one end of the first floor, boasting a tray ceiling, a walk-in closet and a fine bath. Upstairs, a balcony hall overlooks the great room on its way to attic storage to the left and two bedrooms on the right. ©1996 Donald A. Gardner Architects, Inc.

First Floor: 1,585 square feet
Second Floor: 617 square feet
Total: 2,202 square feet

Bonus Room: 353 square feet
Width: 65'-8" Depth: 42'-6"

DESIGN HPT880082

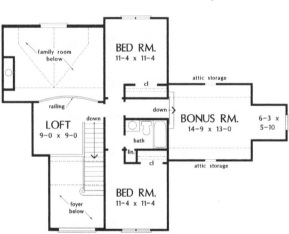

family room below

BED RM.
11-4 x 11-4

attic storage

railing

LOFT
9-0 x 9-0

down

down

BONUS RM.
14-9 x 13-0

6-3 x
5-10

bath

lin.

cl

attic storage

BED RM.
11-4 x 11-4

foyer below

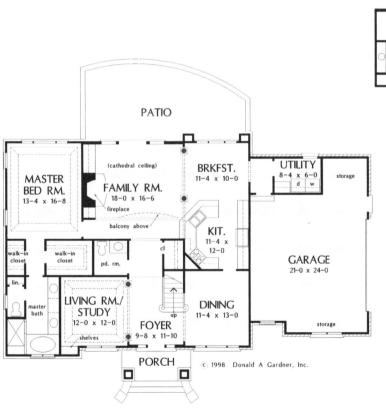

PATIO

MASTER
BED RM.
13-4 x 16-8

(cathedral ceiling)

FAMILY RM.
18-0 x 16-6

fireplace

balcony above

BRKFST.
11-4 x 10-0

UTILITY
8-4 x 6-0

d   w

storage

KIT.
11-4 x
12-0

GARAGE
21-0 x 24-0

walk-in
closet

walk-in
closet

pd. rm.

cl

lin.

master
bath

LIVING RM./
STUDY
12-0 x 12-0

shelves

up

FOYER
9-8 x 11-10

DINING
11-4 x 13-0

storage

PORCH

© 1998   Donald A Gardner, Inc.

Columns, gables, multi-pane windows and a stone and stucco exterior give this home its handsome appearance. The interior amenities are just as impressive. The formal rooms are to the right and left of the foyer with a powder room and coat closet down the hall. The family room, with a cathedral ceiling, fireplace, built-ins and access to the rear patio, is open to the breakfast room through a pair of decorative columns. On the opposite side of the plan, the master suite offers two walk-in closets and a compartmented bath. Two family bedrooms on the second floor share a bath and a loft that overlooks the family room.

First Floor: 1,701 square feet
Second Floor: 534 square feet
Total: 2,235 square feet

Bonus Room: 274 square feet
Width: 65'-11"   Depth: 43'-5"

European Sophistication

Keystone arches, gables and stucco give European sophistication to this great plan, designed for the comfort of today's family. The floor plan begins with a large great room with a fireplace, while a U-shaped kitchen and large utility room stand efficiently nearby. An octagonal tray ceiling dresses up the dining room. Other special ceiling treatments include a cathedral ceiling in the great room and trays in both the master and front bedrooms. An indulgent master bath features a garden tub, a separate shower and dual vanities.

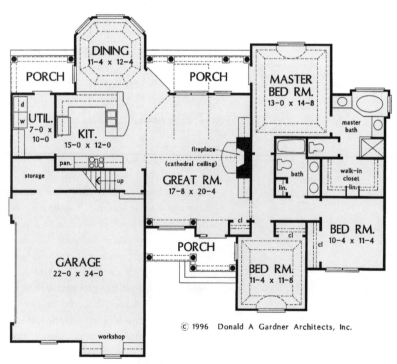

© 1996 Donald A Gardner Architects, Inc.

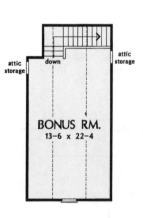

Square Footage: 1,699
Bonus Room: 386 square feet

Width: 63'-8" Depth: 55'-2"

DESIGN HPT880084

Old World Elements

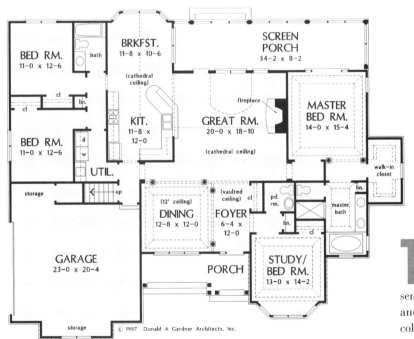

BED RM.
11-0 x 12-6

bath

BRKFST.
11-8 x 10-6

(cathedral ceiling)

SCREEN PORCH
34-2 x 8-2

fireplace

MASTER BED RM.
14-0 x 15-4

KIT.
11-8 x 12-0

GREAT RM.
20-0 x 18-10

(cathedral ceiling)

BED RM.
11-0 x 12-6

UTIL.

storage

up

(12' ceiling)

(vaulted ceiling) cl

pd. rm.

lin.

walk-in closet

master bath

DINING
12-8 x 12-0

FOYER
6-4 x 12-0

lin.

cl

GARAGE
23-0 x 20-4

PORCH

STUDY/ BED RM.
13-0 x 14-2

storage

© 1997 Donald A Gardner Architects, Inc.

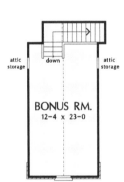

attic storage

down

attic storage

BONUS RM.
12-4 x 23-0

The combination of stone, stucco and windows topped by keystone arches provide this home with Old World elements. The home has a sense of spaciousness, thanks to cathedral ceilings and a minimum of interior walls. Decorative columns separate the dining room from the great room, which offers a fireplace and access to the screened porch. A well-planned kitchen boasts wrapping counters, a cathedral ceiling and a spacious breakfast nook with a bay window. The master suite is positioned for privacy, with two family bedrooms located on the opposite side of the plan.

Square Footage: 2,282
Bonus Room: 354 square feet

Width: 71'-1" Depth: 57'-5"

Raised-Hearth Fireplace

Keystone arches, small-pane windows, chimney design and the stucco exterior combine to give this home a European look. Arches are found inside also, helping to define the boundaries of the foyer, dining room and great room. Noteworthy features of this open area include a raised-hearth fireplace in the great room and an elegant window in the dining room. Another large window illuminates the vaulted living room which could serve instead as a secluded study. Sleeping quarters include a deluxe master suite with His and Hers walk-in closets, a luxurious corner tub and a dual-bowl vanity. Two family bedrooms, a bath and a bonus room complete the plan.

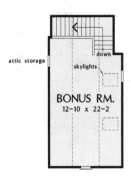

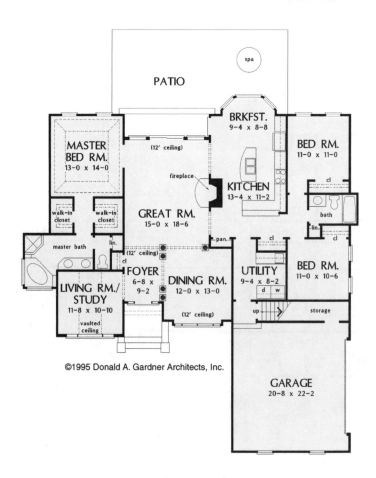

Square Footage: 1,899
Bonus Space: 347 square feet

Width: 60'-0" Depth: 61'-10"

Breath of Fresh Air

SITTING
9-4 x 4-4

PATIO

BRKFST.
9-4 x 10-4

PORCH

storage

MASTER
BED RM.
14-0 x 16-0

FAMILY RM.
21-8 x 15-10

(two story
ceiling)

fireplace

KITCHEN
12-8 x 11-8

bath

master
bath

cl

up

cl

cl

pd.
rm.

BED RM./
OFFICE
11-4 x 12-0

walk-in
closet

lin.

UTIL.
6-0 x
8-0

walk-in
closet

storage

LIVING RM./
STUDY
14-0 x 12-8

fireplace

FOYER
8-8 x
9-0

DINING
12-8 x 13-8

© 1997 DONALD A. GARDNER
All rights reserved

PORCH

GARAGE
24-4 x 20-4

storage

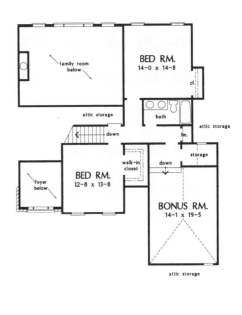

family room
below

BED RM.
14-0 x 14-8

cl

attic storage

bath

attic storage

down

lin.

foyer
below

BED RM.
12-8 x 13-8

walk-in
closet

storage

down

BONUS RM.
14-1 x 19-5

attic storage

Warmth personified, this stucco-and-stone beauty is like a breath of fresh air from the countryside of France. The plan is accommodating without being stuffy. Space for formal occasions opens the plan, including a living room (or make it a study) with a fireplace and the formal dining room. The large family room opens to a rear patio—here's where family members will spend their time. The first-floor master suite is appointed with a sitting area and fine bath. An additional bedroom on this level makes a fine guest bedroom or a home office. The second floor holds two family bedrooms and a full bath. There is also bonus space on this floor (down a few steps) for an additional bedroom or a hobby room.

First Floor: 2,293 square feet
Second Floor: 623 square feet
Total: 2,916 square feet

Bonus Room: 359 square feet
Width: 65'-4" Depth: 63'-0"

Wide-Open Spaces

DESIGN HPT880087

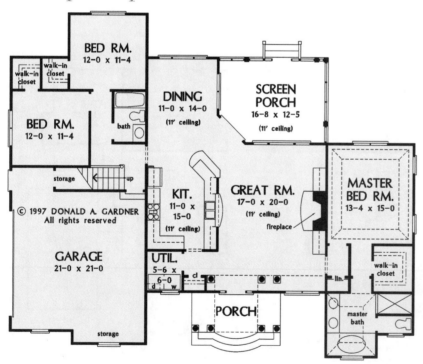

BED RM.
12–0 x 11–4

walk-in closet

walk-in closet

DINING
11–0 x 14–0
(11' ceiling)

SCREEN PORCH
16–8 x 12–5
(11' ceiling)

bath

BED RM.
12–0 x 11–4

storage   up

KIT.
11–0 x 15–0
(11' ceiling)

GREAT RM.
17–0 x 20–0
(11' ceiling)

fireplace

MASTER BED RM.
13–4 x 15–0

GARAGE
21–0 x 21–0

UTIL.
5–6 x 6–0

cl

lin.

walk-in closet

PORCH

d   w

master bath

storage

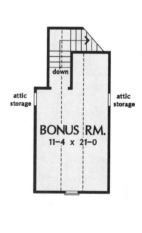

down

attic storage

attic storage

BONUS RM.
11–4 x 21–0

Though tending toward Spanish-style, this home carries a more classic, formal look than the traditional Mediterranean of its genre. More symmetrical than most, it offers a raised porch with columns and multi-pane windows with detailing. The interior is pure modern floor planning. The living areas are open, with eleven foot ceilings and an easy flow from great room to din-ing room to kitchen. The rear screened porch supplies outdoor liv-ing. The bedrooms have the popular split-style arrangement seen in many new homes. The master suite features a tray ceiling, walk-in closet and grandly appointed master bath. Two family bedrooms have walk-in closets and share a full bath.

Square Footage: 1,782
Bonus Room: 229 square feet

Width: 64'-5" **Depth:** 52'-11"

Stucco, Stone and Cedar

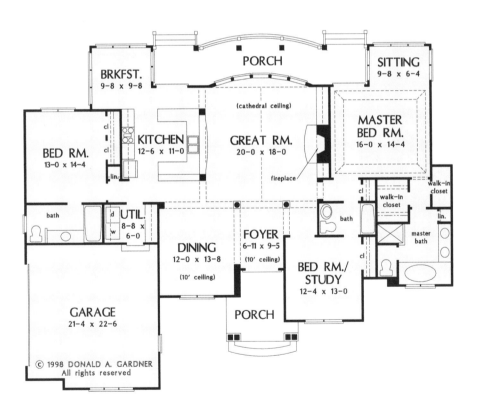

Featuring a stunning exterior of stucco, stone and cedar shakes, this home both blends with and takes advantage of the beauty of its natural surroundings. Designed for optimum openness, the common areas are defined by interior columns and ceiling heights. Windows extend dramatically across the back of the home for exceptional backyard views. The master suite features a tray ceiling, sitting alcove, and private bath with dual walk-in closets, garden tub and separate shower. A bedroom/study, located adjacent to the master suite, has access to a hall bath, and a third bedroom on the opposite of the home boasts its own private bath.

Square Footage: 2,201   Width: 69'-6" Depth: 55'-10"

© 1996 Donald A Gardner Architects, Inc.

21st-Century Floor Plan

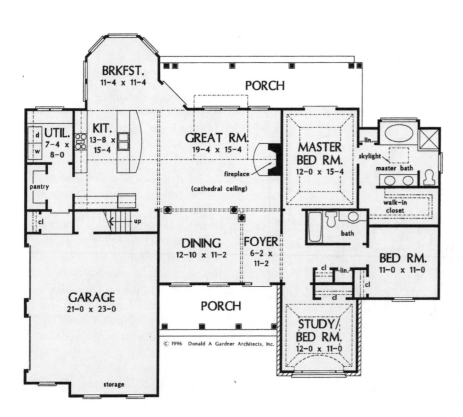

BRKFST.
11-4 x 11-4

PORCH

UTIL.
7-4 x
8-0

KIT.
13-8 x
15-4

pantry

GREAT RM.
19-4 x 15-4

MASTER
BED RM.
12-0 x 15-4

fireplace

(cathedral ceiling)

lin.

skylight

master bath

walk-in
closet

DINING
12-10 x 11-2

FOYER
6-2 x
11-2

up

bath

BED RM.
11-0 x 11-0

GARAGE
21-0 x 23-0

PORCH

cl lin.

cl

STUDY/
BED RM.
12-0 x 11-0

storage

© 1996 Donald A Gardner Architects, Inc.

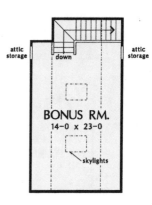

attic
storage

down

attic
storage

BONUS RM.
14-0 x 23-0

skylights

An appealing blend of stone, siding and stucco announces a 21st-Century floor plan that invites traditional events as well as cozy family gatherings. A formal dining area defined by decorative columns opens to a grand great room with wide views of the outdoors. The gourmet kitchen overlooks an expansive food-preparation counter to the great room, and enjoys natural light brought in by the bayed breakfast nook. The sleeping wing, to the right of the plan, includes a sumptuous master suite with a tray ceiling, a door to the rear property, and a skylit bath with twin vanities and a walk-in closet. A secluded study neighbors a family bedroom and shares its bath.

Square Footage: 1,912
Bonus Room: 398 square feet

Width: 67'-7" Depth: 56'-7"

DESIGN HPT880090

Magnificent Master Suite

A lovely courtyard precedes a grand French-door entry with an arched transom, while stone and stucco accent the exterior of this dignified French country home. The foyer, great room and dining room feature stately eleven-foot ceilings, and interior columns mark boundaries for the great room and dining room. The spacious kitchen features a pass-through to the great room, where built-in shelves flank the fireplace. Cozy side patios and a back porch add to this home's appeal. The master suite is magnificent with a double-door entry, an elegant tray ceiling, dual walk-in closets and an extravagant bath.

Square Footage: 2,250

Width: 84'-10" Depth: 62'-4"

Spacious Dining Room

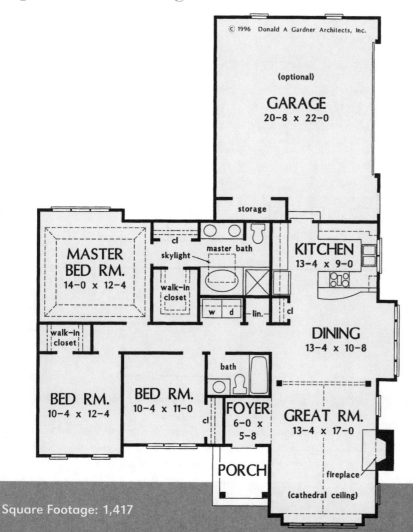

© 1996 Donald A Gardner Architects, Inc.

(optional)

GARAGE
20-8 x 22-0

storage

cl

skylight

master bath

walk-in closet

w   d   lin.   cl

MASTER BED RM.
14-0 x 12-4

walk-in closet

KITCHEN
13-4 x 9-0

DINING
13-4 x 10-8

bath

BED RM.
10-4 x 12-4

BED RM.
10-4 x 11-0

cl

FOYER
6-0 x 5-8

GREAT RM.
13-4 x 17-0

fireplace

PORCH

(cathedral ceiling)

Stucco siding and box-bay windows add special delights to this one-story European home. The floor plan has an open, airy feeling with a cathedral ceiling and a colonnaded opening in the great room. The fireplace adds warmth and coziness to the entire common area. There is a tray ceiling in the master bedroom, which also features two closets and a skylit bath with every indulgence. Two family bedrooms share the use of a hall bath. Across the hall are a laundry alcove and linen closet.

Square Footage: 1,417

Width: 46'-0" Depth: 39'-0"

DESIGN HPT880092

This home is dressed to impress with its stone and stucco exterior and dramatic square-columned entry. The great room with cathedral ceiling adjoins a breakfast area which opens onto a side porch. The kitchen features a pantry and an angled counter with stovetop. A separate utility room has built-in cabinets and a countertop with laundry sink. Double doors lead into the first-floor master suite with box-bay window, two walk-in closets and a lavish bath. Two more bedrooms are located upstairs, along with a full bath, a linen closet and a skylit bonus room.

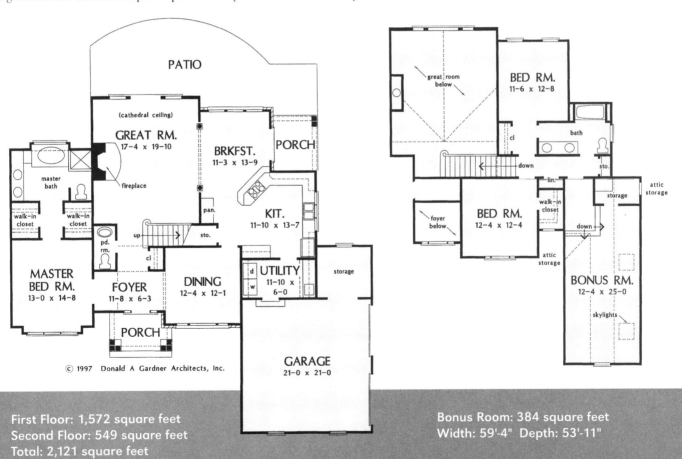

© 1997 Donald A Gardner Architects, Inc.

First Floor: 1,572 square feet
Second Floor: 549 square feet
Total: 2,121 square feet

Bonus Room: 384 square feet
Width: 59'-4" Depth: 53'-11"

Compact Traditional Home

An elegant brick column helps frame the welcoming front porch, while eye-catching window designs help maximize the street appeal of this compact traditional home. The interior of this design is equally appealing. A formal dining room opens to the left of the entrance foyer and is well served by the adjacent kitchen with its convenient cooktop island. A sunny breakfast area overlooks the rear of the property and accesses the back patio. The heart of the house will be the family room, which boasts a twelve-foot ceiling, a cozy brick fireplace and two sets of French doors to outdoor living areas. Two large family bedrooms share a full hall bath, and the master suite pampers with a walk-in closet and twin lavs.

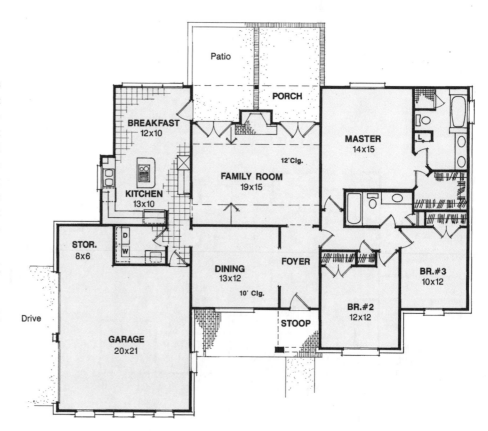

Square Footage: 1,739

Width: 64'-0" Depth: 49'-0"

DESIGN HPT880094

Pampering Bath

With a decidedly European flavor, this two-story home features family living at its best. The foyer opens to a study or living room on the left. The dining room on the right offers large proportions and full windows. The family room remains open to the kitchen and the breakfast room. Here, sunny meals are guaranteed with a bay window overlooking the rear yard. In the master suite, a bayed sitting area, a walk-in closet and a pampering bath are sure to please. Upstairs, two family bedrooms flank a loft or study area.

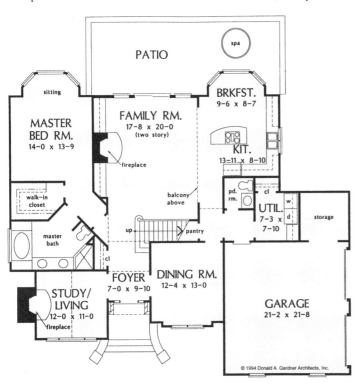

© 1994 Donald A. Gardner Architects, Inc.

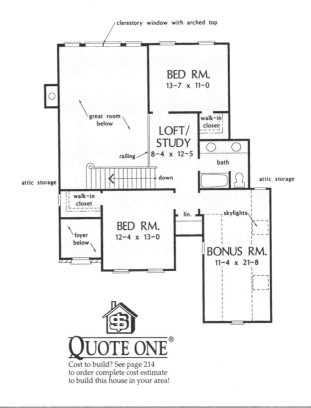

QUOTE ONE®
Cost to build? See page 214 to order complete cost estimate to build this house in your area!

First Floor: 1,715 square feet
Second Floor: 620 square feet
Total: 2,335 square feet

Bonus Room: 265 square feet
Width: 58'-6" Depth: 50'-3"

Splendid Colonnade

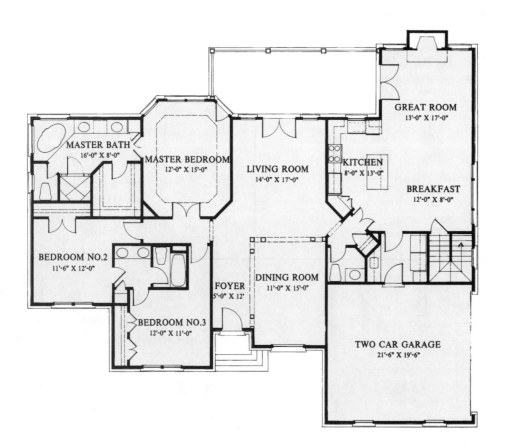

GREAT ROOM
13'-0" X 17'-0"

MASTER BATH
16'-0" X 8'-0"

MASTER BEDROOM
12'-0" X 15'-0"

LIVING ROOM
14'-0" X 17'-0"

KITCHEN
8'-0" X 13'-0"

BREAKFAST
12'-0" X 8'-0"

BEDROOM NO.2
11'-6" X 12'-0"

FOYER
5'-0" X 12'

DINING ROOM
11'-0" X 15'-0"

BEDROOM NO.3
12'-0" X 11'-0"

TWO CAR GARAGE
21'-6" X 19'-6"

This American classic begins with a recessed entry that announces a modern interior designed for entertaining as well as relaxed gatherings. The foyer leads to the living room, which opens through French doors to the back property, and to a banquet-sized dining room, defined by a splendid colonnade. The spacious kitchen has a work island and a sunlit breakfast area that shares the warmth of a hearth in the great room. French doors open to the master suite, which features a lovely bay window and a lavish bath. This home is designed with a walkout basement foundation.

Square Footage: 2,077

Width: 66'-0" Depth: 54'-0"

DESIGN HPT880096

Cozy Keeping Room

QUOTE ONE®

Cost to build? See page 214
to order complete cost estimate
to build this house in your area!

From the arched covered entry to the jack-arch window, this house retains the distinction of a much larger home. From the foyer and across the spacious great room, French doors and large side windows give a generous view of the covered rear porch. The dining room is subtly defined by the use of columns and a large triple window. The kitchen has a generous work island and breakfast area and joins the cozy keeping room. Two family bedrooms share a private bath. The home is completed by a quiet master suite located at the rear. It contains a bay window, a garden tub and His and Hers vanities. This home is designed with a walkout basement foundation.

Square Footage: 2,150

Width: 64'-0" Depth: 60'-4"

Formal Living and Dining Rooms

Depending on European and French influences for its exterior beauty, this regal home belies the theory that a single-story design has no character. A volume roofline helps make the difference, both inside and out, allowing for vaulted ceilings in many of the interior spaces. There are more than enough living areas in this plan: formal living and dining rooms, a huge family room with a fireplace, and a study with a bay window. The kitchen features an attached, light-filled breakfast area. Two family bedrooms on the right side of the plan share a full bath, while the third family bathroom has a private bath. The master suite has a private covered patio, a vaulted ceiling, two walk-in closets and a bath fit for a king.

Square Footage: 3,056

Width: 80'-0" Depth: 79'-9"

DESIGN HPT880098

European Charm

FAMILY ROOM
15-4 X 16-0
12 FT VAULTED CLG

COVERED PORCH

MASTER BATH

LIVING ROOM
17-0 X 16-0
12 FT CLG

BEDRM 4/STUDY
13-4 X 14-8
10 FT CLG

MASTER BEDROOM
15-4 X 15-4
12 FT TRAY CLG

BRKFST RM
15-4 X 7-6
12 FT VAULTED CLG

42" LEDGE

UP

DOWN

KITCHEN

15-4 X 16-4
10 FT CLG

DINING ROOM
12-8 X 14-4
12 FT CLG

FOYER
12 FT CLG

PWDR

BATH 2

UTIL

PAN

PORCH

BEDROOM 3
12-4 X 13-6
10 FT CLG

BEDROOM 2
12-8 X 12-6
10 FT CLG

GARAGE

A gentle European charm flavors the facade of this ultra-modern home. The foyer opens to a formal dining room, which leads to the kitchen through privacy doors. Here, a center cooktop island complements wrapping counter space, a walk-in pantry and a snack counter. Casual living space shares a through-fireplace with the formal living room and provides its own access to the rear porch. Clustered sleeping quarters include a well-appointed master suite, two family bedrooms and an additional bedroom which could double as a study. Please specify basement, crawlspace or slab foundation when ordering.

Square Footage: 2,745

Width: 69'-6" Depth: 76'-8"

Unique Ceiling Treatments

There's nowhere to go but up in this bright and airy three-bedroom home. Nearly every room has a unique ceiling treatment, including the living room, dining room, breakfast nook, master suite and T-shaped secondary bedroom on the second floor. The living room features a grand hearth. Another fireplace is located in the comfortable great room. The dining room is easily accessed by a uniquely designed kitchen which provides extra counter space. The breakfast nook is flooded by natural light and allows access to the backyard. The upstairs loft overlooks main-floor action below. Two family bedrooms are kept on the second level as well as attic storage space. This home is designed with a walkout basement foundation.

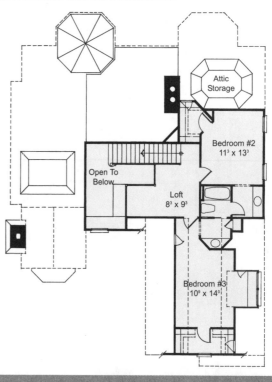

First Floor: 1,724 square feet
Second Floor: 700 square feet
Total: 2,424 square feet

Width: 47'-10" Depth: 63'-6"

Future Expansion

Multi-pane windows, shutters and shingle accents adorn the stucco facade of this wonderful French country home. Inside, the foyer introduces the hearth-warmed great room that features French-door access to the rear deck. The dining room, defined from the foyer and great room by columns, enjoys front-yard views. The master bedroom includes two walk-in closets, rear-deck access and a dual vanity bath. The informal living areas have an open plan. The box-bayed breakfast nook joins the cooktop-island kitchen and hearth-warmed family room. The second floor holds two bedrooms with walk-in closets, a study and an unfinished bedroom for future expansion.

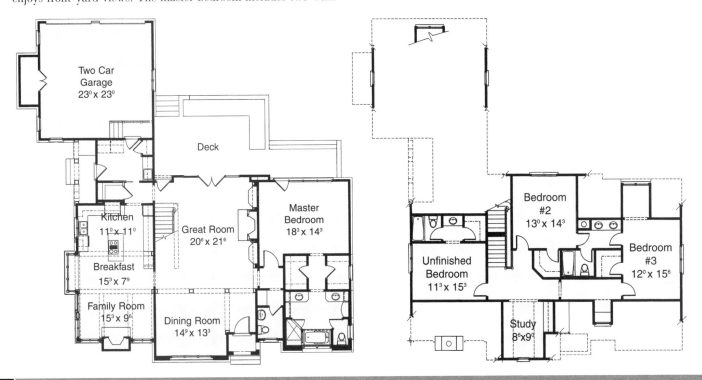

First Floor: 1,840 square feet
Second Floor: 840 square feet
Total: 2,680 square feet

Bonus Space: 295 square feet
Width: 66'-0" **Depth:** 65'-10"

Sensational Sun Room

Deck

Sun Room
16⁴x9¹⁰

Master Bedroom
16⁴x18⁴

Breakfast
11⁶x14⁰

Great Room
19⁸x15⁰

Kitchen
12⁴x15⁰

Bedroom No. 2
12⁰x13⁰

Study
11⁴x14⁰

Dining Room
11⁰x16⁰

Two Car Garage
21⁴x21⁶

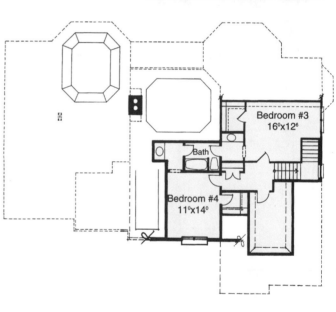

Bedroom #3
16⁰x12⁶

Bath

Bedroom #4
11⁰x14⁰

Stone and stucco bring a chateau welcome to this Mediterranean-style home. A sensational sun room lights up the rear of the plan and flows to the bayed breakfast nook. A coffered ceiling and columned archways decorate the living area, which opens to the formal dining room. A master suite with rear-deck access leads to a family or guest bedroom with a private bath. Upstairs, two secondary bedrooms and a full bath enjoy easy kitchen access down a side stairway. This home is designed with a walkout basement foundation.

First Floor: 2,502 square feet
Second Floor: 677 square feet
Total: 3,179 square feet

Bonus Space: 171 square feet
Width: 71'-2" Depth: 56'-10"

DESIGN HPT880102

Great Covered Porch

Imagine the luxurious living you'll enjoy in this beautiful home! The natural beauty of stone combined with sophisticated window detailing represent the good taste you'll find carried throughout the design. Common living areas occupy the center of the plan and include the great room with a fireplace, the sun room and the breakfast area, plus rear and side porches. A second fireplace is located in the front den. The master suite features private access to the rear porch and a wonderfully planned bath. This home is designed with a walkout basement foundation.

Square Footage: 2,140

Width: 62'-0" Depth: 60'-6"

Great for Entertaining

From the street, the high-pitched rooflines, stucco turrets and stone detailing make this residence very elegant. The great room provides flexibility in a layout that's great for entertaining and everday living. The built-ins and fireplace create an exciting focal point here. Large sliding glass doors pocket into the wall, opening the living room up to the outdoor covered lanai. The formal dining room is detailed by arches in columns. The oversized kitchen contains a walk-in pantry, an eating bar and an island cooktop. Two bedrooms have plenty of closet space and share a bath that accesses the outdoor lanai and grill area. The master wing includes a study, access to the lanai, two walk-in closets, His and Hers vanity areas and a dressing space.

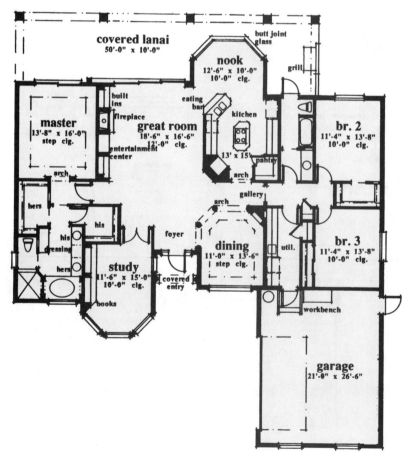

Square Footage: 2,431

Width: 65'-0" Depth: 74'-6"

DESIGN HPT880104

Quiet Study with Fireplace

Deck

Breakfast
13³ x 10⁰

Kitchen
13³ x 16⁰

Great
Room
14⁶ x 19⁰

Master
Bedroom
13³ x 17⁹

Two Car
Garage
21³ x 21⁶

Dining
Room
12⁰ x 16⁰

Study
11³ x 15³

Bedroom
No. 4
13³ x 11³

Open To
Below

Bedroom
No. 3
15⁰ x 12⁰

Bedroom
No. 2
12³ x 13⁶

Open To
Below

Open To
Below

To the left of the recessed entry foyer, the box-windowed formal dining room leads to a large L-shaped kitchen with a separate utility area, an island cooktop and a sunny breakfast bay with deck access. The great room features a fireplace and rear access through French doors. To the right of the foyer is a quiet study with another fireplace. The lavish master suite includes a bay-windowed sitting area, an elegant tray ceiling and a private bath with dual walk-in closets and vanities, a separate shower and a whirlpool tub. Two of the three second-floor bedrooms include walk-in closets. This home is designed with a walkout basement foundation.

First Floor: 1,932 square feet
Second Floor: 807 square feet
Total: 2,739 square feet

Width: 63'-0" Depth: 51'-6"

Rear View

Sunshine and Views

4,50 X 4,50
15'-0" X 15'-0"

1,90 X 4,00
6'-4" X 13'-4"

3,30 X 3,60
11'-0" X 12'-0"

3,60 X 4,50
12'-0" X 15'-0"

4,10 X 3,00
13'-8" X 10'-0"

6,90 X 6,30
23'-0" X 21'-0"

3,00 X 3,00
10'-0" X 10'-0"

3,00 X 3,30
10'-0" X 11'-0"

OPEN TO BELOW

3,30 X 3,60
11'-0" X 12'-0"

BONUS ROOM
6,10 X 4,20
20'-4" X 14'-0"

4,20 X 3,00
14'-0" X 10'-0"

Front View

A plenitude of windows provides both sunshine and views for this attractive three-bedroom home. Just off the foyer, an office/study awaits. At the rear of the home, a spacious two-story living area features a warming fireplace and easy access to the dining area and kitchen. This room offers sliding glass doors to a private dining patio as well as to your own greenhouse! Secluded on the first floor, the master suite is complete with a walk-in closet, dual vanities and separate tub and shower. This home is designed with a basement foundation.

First Floor: 1,525 square feet
Second Floor: 470 square feet
Total: 1,995 square feet

Width: 56'-0" Depth: 53'-2"

Rear View

DESIGN HPT880106

Great Views

Perfect for waterfront property, this home boasts windows everywhere. Inside, open planning can be found in the living room, which offers a corner fireplace for cool evenings and blends beautifully into the dining and kitchen areas. All areas enjoy windowed views. A laundry room is conveniently nestled between the kitchen and the two-car garage. The master suite features a walk-through closet and sumptuous bath. Upstairs, three uniquely shaped bedrooms share a full bath. This home is designed with a basement foundation.

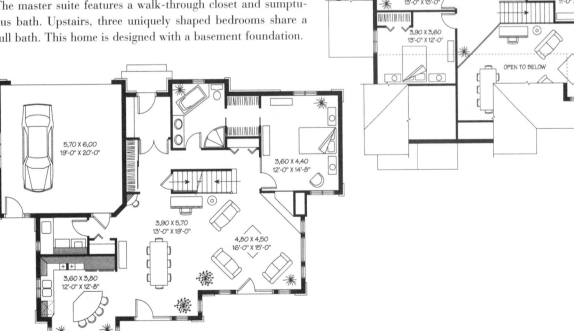

First Floor: 1,324 square feet
Second Floor: 688 square feet
Total: 2,012 square feet

Width: 55'-0" Depth: 41'-0"

See-Through Fireplace

DESIGN HPT880107

The farmhouse appeal of this four-bedroom home is in the wrapping, covered porch—perfect for rocking away the afternoons. The exterior detailing adds the look of yesteryear, but the inside floor plan brings things up-to-date. You can easily unload a station wagon full of groceries using the quick path from garage to kitchen and then warm up by the see-through fireplace. The spacious great room is enhanced by a bay window and shares the through-fireplace with the kitchen. Upstairs, four bedrooms include a pampering master suite. The master bath includes His and Hers sinks, tub, separate shower and spacious walk-in closet.

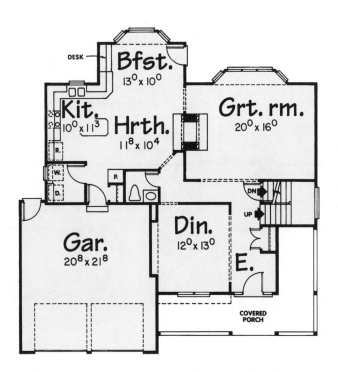

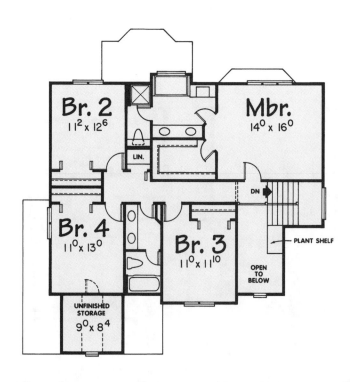

First Floor: 1,158 square feet
Second Floor: 1,134 square feet
Total: 2,292 square feet

Width: 46'-0" Depth: 47'-10"

DESIGN HPT880108

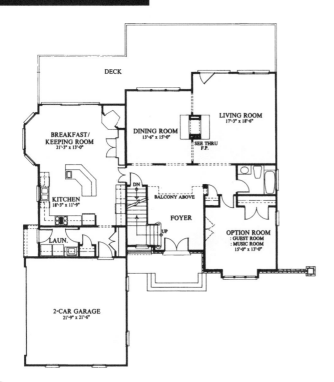

DECK

BREAKFAST/ KEEPING ROOM 21'-3" x 13'-0"

DINING ROOM 13'-6" x 15'-0"

LIVING ROOM 17'-3" x 18'-6"

SEE THRU F.P.

KITCHEN 18'-3" x 11'-9"

DN

BALCONY ABOVE

FOYER

UP

OPTION ROOM : GUEST ROOM : MUSIC ROOM 15'-0" x 13'-0"

LAUN.

2-CAR GARAGE 21'-9" x 21'-6"

HIS

HERS

M. BATH

MASTER SUITE 17'-3" x 18'-6"

SEE THRU F.P.

BEDROOM No.3 13'-3" x 12'-0"

DN

OPEN TO BELOW

BEDROOM No.2 15'-0" x 13'-3"

VLT.CLG.

UNFINISHED STORAGE 11'-0" x 21'-9"

opping the arched entry of this home is a lovely transom window, which admits sunlight to enhance the magnificence of the two-story foyer. The formal atmosphere of the living and dining rooms is brought together by a through-fireplace. Generously sized windows in these rooms allow views of outside living areas or children's play areas. An additional fireplace can be found in the corner of the keeping room, adjacent to the enormous kitchen and the breakfast area, which is set off by a bay window. The master suite features an expansive master bath with a large walk-in closet. This home is designed with a walkout basement foundation.

First Floor: 1,811 square feet
Second Floor: 1,437 square feet
Total: 3,248 square feet

Bonus Space: 286 square feet
Width: 53'-6" Depth: 60'-6"

Wraparound Porch

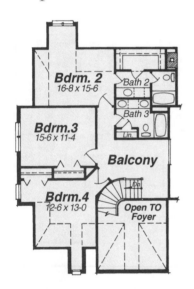

Bdrm. 2
16-8 x 15-6

Bath 2

Bath 3

Lin.

Bdrm.3
15-6 x 11-4

Balcony

Bdrm.4
12-6 x 13-0

Open TO
Foyer

Sundeck
12-0 x 12-0

Vault

Sunroom
15-4 x 11-6

Sundeck
24-0 x 12-0

Kit.
12-0 x 15-6

Dw. Ref.

Breakfast/
Keeping
17-0 x 15-6

Dining
13-0 x 15-6

China

China

W.D.

Laund.
10-0 x 9-6

Ov.

Pant.

Fr.

Double Garage
21-4 x 23-4

Lav.

M.Bath

C.

Courtyard

Living Area
21-0 x 17-4

Line Of
Balcony

Master
Bdrm.
15-6 x 17-6

Open
Foyer
13-6 x 13-6

Line Of
Balcony

Built in

Media
13-6 x 13-6

Porch

This charming home boasts a wraparound porch, a sun room, two decks and a courtyard. Beyond the stately Palladian entrance, the two-story foyer is roomy enough to be furnished. Straight ahead, a hall leads to the heart of the home—kitchen, breakfast area and keeping room with fireplace. A formal dining room is adjacent and close to a large living area with another fireplace. Nestled behind the staircase is the master suite. The master bathroom features a corner garden tub, two vanities and access to a large walk-in closet. Upstairs are three additional bedrooms.

First Floor: 2,380 square feet
Second Floor: 1,086 square feet
Total: 3,466 square feet

Width: 85'-0" Depth: 70'-0"

Homes in the
English Tradition

To view floor plans,
see page 27.

Spacious Great Room

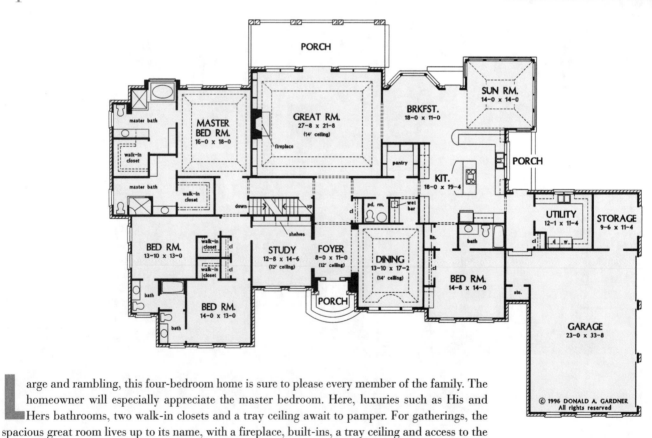

Large and rambling, this four-bedroom home is sure to please every member of the family. The homeowner will especially appreciate the master bedroom. Here, luxuries such as His and Hers bathrooms, two walk-in closets and a tray ceiling await to pamper. For gatherings, the spacious great room lives up to its name, with a fireplace, built-ins, a tray ceiling and access to the rear porch. The kitchen features an island cooktop/snack bar, a walk-in pantry and an adjacent bayed breakfast room. A sun room is also nearby. Note the storage in the three-car garage.

Square Footage: 4,523

Width: 114'-4" Depth: 82'-3"

DESIGN HPT880111

This home combines the rustic charm of shutters and a random stonework wall with the elegance of molded cornices and arched multi-pane windows to create a look all its own. From the nicely detailed covered porch, enter upon the formal dining room to the right and living room to the rear. The arched gallery leads past the kitchen with island and bar to the family room with fireplace and built-in entertainment center. Adjoining the kitchen and family room is the bay-windowed breakfast nook which looks out onto the rear patio. Three family bedrooms are located to the front. Bedroom 4 offers a private bath, while Bedrooms 2 and 3 share a full bath that includes separate vanities.

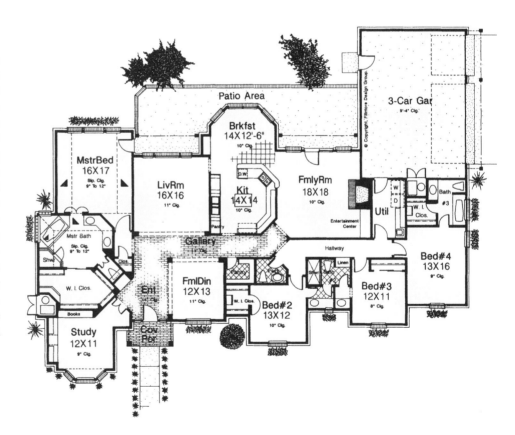

Square Footage: 3,352

Width: 91'-0" Depth: 71'-9"

Fine Wood Detailing

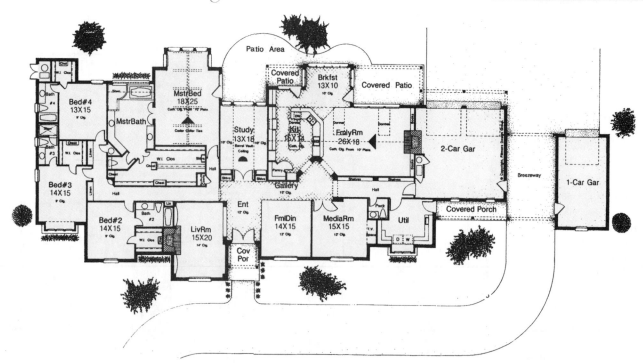

Here is a home fit for a king or for the lord of any manor. In this English country design, a series of hip roofs covers an impressive brick facade accented by fine wood detailing. You will entertain in style in formal living and dining rooms that flank the foyer and in the nearby media room, designed for home theater and surround sound. Fireplaces warm the living room and the family room, which also boasts a cathedral ceiling. The kitchen offers plenty of work space, a bright breakfast nook and access to two covered patios. Convenient to all areas of the house, the barrel-vaulted study has a wall of windows and French doors that can be closed for private meetings or quiet relaxing.

Square Footage: 4,825

Width: 155'-6" Depth: 60'-4"

DESIGN HPT880114

Two Covered Patios

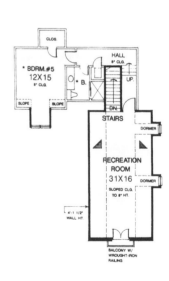

A unique entrance made of rough cedar offers a warm welcome to this brick English-style country home. A large study to the left of the entry features a fireplace and a vaulted ceiling, and would function well as a home office. Formal living and dining rooms are diagonally across from each other, with the U-shaped kitchen nearby. The family room, sporting a cathedral ceiling and a fireplace, and the breakfast nook complete the indoor living area. Two covered patios add outdoor possibilities. The sleeping zone is split, with three family bedrooms and two baths to the right of the plan, and the master suite, with a fine bath and a bayed sitting area, to the left. Upstairs, an outdoor balcony opens off a recreation room.

First Floor: 3,957 square feet
Second Floor: 515 square feet
Total: 4,472 square feet

Width: 89'-10" Depth: 78'-10"

Envy of Your Guests

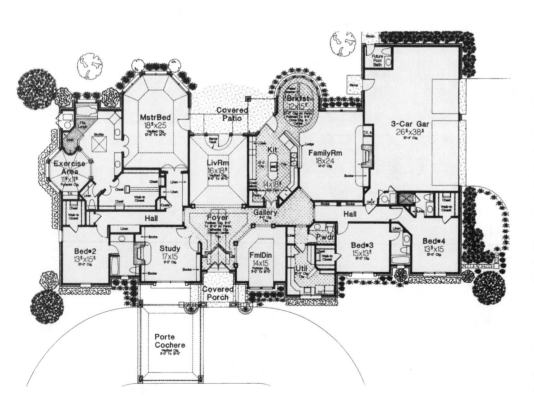

The hipped-roof, French-country exterior and porte-cochere entrance are just the beginning of this unique and impressive design. An unusual Pullman ceiling graces the foyer as it leads to the formal dining room on the right, to the study with a fireplace on the left and straight ahead to the formal living room with its covered patio access. A gallery directs you to the island kitchen with its abundant counter space and adjacent sun-filled breakfast bay. On the left side of the home, a spectacular master suite will become your favorite haven and the envy of your guests. The master bedroom includes a coffered ceiling, a bayed sitting area and patio access. The master bath features a large doorless shower, a separate exercise room and a huge walk-in closet with built-in chests. All of the family bedrooms offer private baths and walk-in closets.

Square Footage: 4,615

Width: 109'-10" Depth: 89'-4"

DESIGN HPT880116

Pampering Master Bath

A brick exterior, stucco, and cedar timbers provide the stately Tudor identity that characterizes this English country home. Making a grand entrance, the two-story entry features a marble floor that leads to formal and informal living areas. An adjacent study warmed by a fireplace provides a quiet place to relax and savor contemplative moments. Located for privacy, the sumptuous master suite contains a pampering master bath and a huge walk-in closet sized for frequent shoppers. Informal gatherings will be enjoyed in the two-story family room overlooking the covered patio and rear grounds. The adjoining breakfast room shares space with a gourmet kitchen that serves formal and informal areas with equal ease. The second floor contains three family bedrooms—each with a walk-in closet—two baths and a large sitting area.

First Floor: 2,736 square feet
Second Floor: 1,276 square feet
Total: 4,012 square feet

Width: 80'-0" Depth: 65'-0"

Dignified Details

DESIGN HPT880117

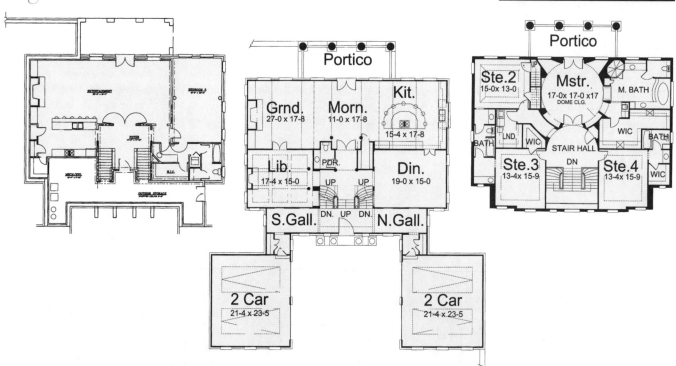

Portico

Grnd.
27-0 x 17-8

Morn.
11-0 x 17-8

Kit.
15-4 x 17-8

Lib.
17-4 x 15-0

PDR.

Din.
19-0 x 15-0

UP   UP

S.Gall.   DN. UP DN.   N.Gall.

2 Car
21-4 x 23-5

2 Car
21-4 x 23-5

Portico

Ste.2
15-0x 13-0

UP

Mstr.
17-0x 17-0 x17
DOME CLG.

M. BATH

BATH   LND.   WIC

WIC

BATH

Ste.3
13-4 x 15-9

STAIR HALL

DN

Ste.4
13-4 x 15-9

WIC

Simply elegant, with dignified details, this beautiful home is reminiscent of English estate homes. Two double garages flank a columned front door and are attached to the main floor by galleries leading to the entry foyer. Here a double staircase leads upstairs and encourages a view beyond the morning room, grand salon and rear portico. The gourmet kitchen has a uniquely styled island counter with a cooktop. For formal meals, the dining hall is nearby. The elaborate master bedroom and three staterooms reside on the second level. The master bedroom features a circular shape and enjoys access to a private lanai, a through-fireplace to the master bath, and numerous alcoves and built-in amenities.

First Floor: 2,175 square feet
Second Floor: 1,927 square feet
Total: 4,102 square feet

Finished Basement: 1,927 square feet
Width: 74'-0" Depth: 82'-0"

DESIGN HPT880118

Magnificent Estate

As you approach this magnificent estate, you will be transformed back in time to the land of gentry. The opulence extends from the circular stairway that floats in front of the grand salon and floor-to-ceiling windows. The dining hall can easily seat twelve with additional furnishings. There is also a butler's pantry on the way to the octagonal kitchen, near a vaulted family room and a vaulted breakfast area. The master suite features all the finest appointments expected in a large home, with built-in dressers, cedar closets, study access, a fireplace, built-ins and massive decorative columns. The second floor has a large stateroom with a sitting room and bath. Two additional staterooms feature private baths.

Second Floor Plan

- SITTING RM — 11'-6" x 14'-0"
- STATEROOM #1 — 15'-3" x 13'-10"
- OPEN TO SALON
- STATEROOM #3 — 14'-6" x 13'-0"
- BATH
- open rail
- dressing
- OPEN TO FOYER
- STATEROOM #2 — 14'-6" x 15'-6"
- GALLERY — 8'-6" x 12'-5"
- window seat
- FUTURE ROOM — 16'-7" x 35'-6"
- 10'-0" clg. ht.

First Floor Plan

- MASTER STATEROOM — 15'-5" x 22'-6", 15'-10" clg. ht.
- FAMILY ROOM — 17'-5" x 21'-0", 18'-10" clg. ht.
- MSTR BATH — 11'-6" x 14'-3"
- GRAND SALON — 18'-0" x 19'-0"
- MORNING ROOM — 19'-1" x 12'-7"
- KITCHEN — 13'-6" x 18'-7"
- PWDR
- HALL
- PANTRY
- FOYER — 18'-3" x 13'-2"
- STUDY — 15'-2" x 11'-4"
- DINING HALL — 15'-6" x 17'-1"
- BUTLER'S PANTRY
- UTILITY
- PORTE COCHERE — 14'-7" x 22'-0"
- 2-CAR GARAGE — 21'-5" x 24'-0"
- DETACHED 2-CAR GARAGE — 21'-6" x 22'-0"
- COVERED PORCH

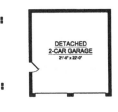

First Floor: 3,103 square feet
Second Floor: 1,482 square feet
Total: 4,585 square feet

Bonus Space: 786 square feet
Width: 106'-0" Depth: 56'-6"

English Country Design

A raised built-up planter and large multi-pane window topped by a keystone arch are special touches on the facade of this English country design. A recessed entry leads to a foyer that is open to the formal dining room and the family room, creating a large area for entertaining. A corner fireplace, built-ins, columned arches and access to the rear terrace highlight the area. An octagonal breakfast nook with an attached screened porch is separated from the kitchen by a snack bar. Nearby are an office, a powder room, a mudroom and laundry facilities. The master suite is on the first floor, with two walk-in closets, a dressing area and a compartmented bath designed to pamper. Family sleeping quarters are upstairs and include four bedrooms and two baths.

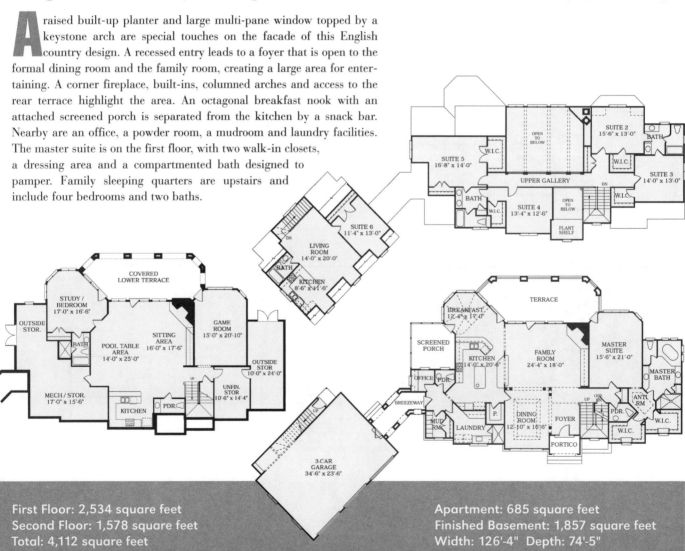

First Floor: 2,534 square feet
Second Floor: 1,578 square feet
Total: 4,112 square feet

Apartment: 685 square feet
Finished Basement: 1,857 square feet
Width: 126'-4" Depth: 74'-5"

DESIGN HPT880120

Cozy Study with Fireplace

Stone and brick combine with gables and arches on the facade of this fine English manor. A grand arched doorway welcomes friends and family alike to this delightful design. Inside, the two-story foyer is flanked by the formal dining room to the left and a cozy study with a fireplace and built-in bookcases to the right. Directly ahead, the great room features a sloped ceiling and a stone hearth. The spacious kitchen offers a worktop island, a walk-in pantry and a serving counter to the sunny breakfast room. Separated for privacy, the first-floor master suite is complete with two walk-in closets, a lavish bath and a private patio area. Upstairs, Bedrooms 3 and 4 share a bath, while Bedroom 2 insists on privacy. The large recreation room is perfect for kids. A three-car garage will easily handle the family fleet.

First Floor: 2,317 square feet
Second Floor: 1,302 square feet
Total: 3,619 square feet

Width: 74'-0" Depth: 56'-4"

Separate Apartment

Be the owner of your own country estate—this two-story home gives the look and feel of grand-style living without the expense of large square footage. The entry leads to a massive foyer and great hall, worthy of your estate lifestyle. There's space enough here for living and dining areas. Two window seats in the great hall overlook the rear veranda. One fireplace warms the living area, while another looks through the dining room to the kitchen and breakfast nook. A screened porch offers casual dining space for warm weather. The master suite has another fireplace and window seat and adjoins a luxurious master bath with separate tub and shower. A separate apartment over the garage includes its own living room, kitchen and bedroom.

Quote One®

Cost to build? See page 214 to order complete cost estimate to build this house in your area!

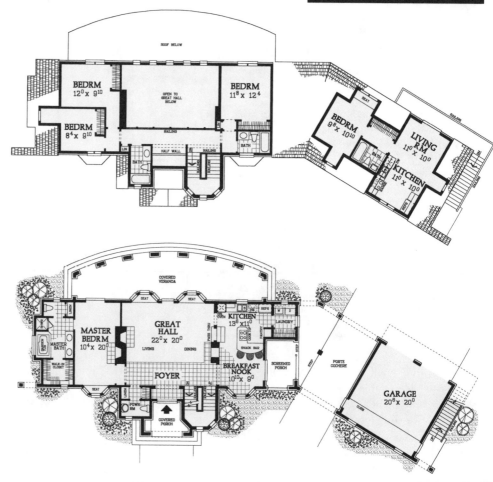

First Floor: 1,566 square feet
Second Floor: 837 square feet
Total: 2,403 square feet

Apartment: 506 square feet
Width: 116'-3" Depth: 55'-1"

L

DESIGN HPT880122

Multiple rooflines, a stone, brick and siding facade and an absolutely grand entrance combine to give this home the look of luxury. A striking family room showcases a beautiful fireplace framed with built-ins. The nearby breakfast room streams with light and accesses the rear patio. The kitchen features an island workstation, walk-in pantry and plenty of counter space. A guest suite is available on the first floor, perfect for when elderly members of the family visit. The master suite, also on the first floor, enjoys easy access to a large study, a bayed sitting room and a luxurious bath. Private baths are also included for each of the upstairs bedrooms.

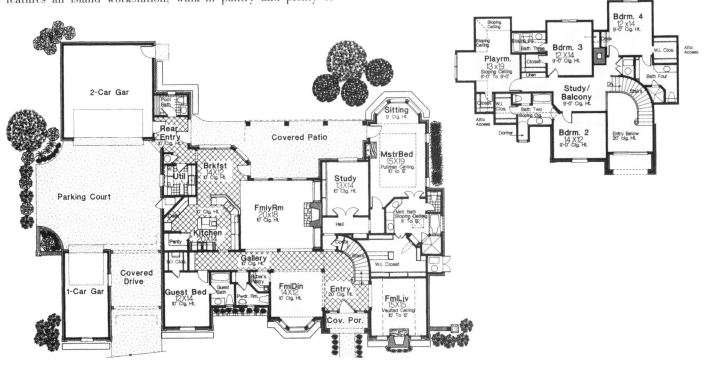

First Floor: 3,248 square feet
Second Floor: 1,426 square feet
Total: 4,674 square feet

Width: 99'-10" Depth: 74'-10"

Floor-to-Ceiling Cabinetry

This stately brick home offers a magnificent elevation from every angle, with a particularly impressive arched portico and quoin trim. The entry hall is highlighted by a majestic staircase ascending to an elegant balcony. The spacious formal dining room includes two built-in china cabinets and is easily reached from the living room with its cheery fireplace and attractive window seat. Between them is a handsomely appoint-ed den with floor-to-ceiling cabinetry, a window seat and a spider-beam ceiling. An expansive gourmet kitchen with a walk-in pantry and an island cooktop/snack bar opens to a distinctive family room featuring a built-in roll-top desk, an entertainment center and a raised-hearth fireplace. The nearby breakfast nook offers panoramic views to the outside.

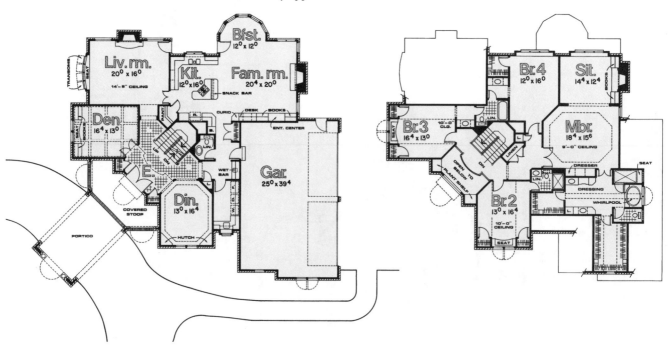

First Floor: 2,040 square feet
Second Floor: 1,952 square feet
Total: 3,992 square feet

Width: 68'-0" Depth: 66'-0"

DESIGN HPT880124

Future Playroom Area

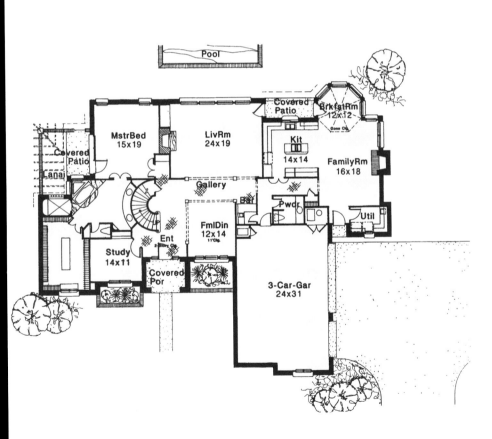

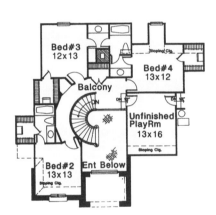

The distinctive covered entry to this stunning manor leads to a gracious entry with impressive two-story semi-circular fanlights. The entry leads to a study, formal dining room, formal living room and master suite. The numerous amenities in the kitchen include an island workstation and built-in pantry. The breakfast room features a cone ceiling. The luxurious master bath, secluded in its own wing, is complete with a covered patio. The master bedroom has a huge walk-in closet. Upstairs are three bedrooms, two baths and a future playroom area.

First Floor: 2,997 square feet
Second Floor: 983 square feet
Total: 3,980 square feet

Playroom: 208 square feet
Width: 89'-4" Depth: 71'-1"

Perfect for Entertaining

Full of amenities, this country estate includes a media room and a study. The two-story great room is perfect for formal entertaining. Family and friends will enjoy gathering in the large kitchen, the hearth room and the breakfast room. The luxurious master suite is located upstairs. Bedrooms 2 and 3 share a bath that includes dressing areas for both bedrooms. Bedroom 4 features a private bath. The detached garage is equipped with stairs to the expandable area above. The home features a walkout basement with an enormous workshop, a game room and a hobby room. Please specify basement or slab foundation when ordering.

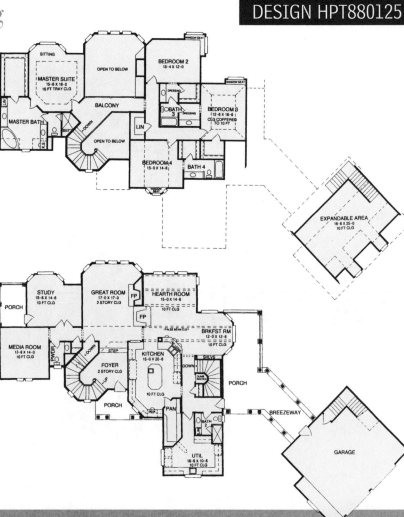

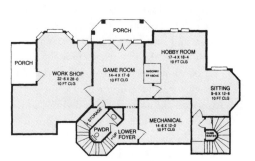

First Floor: 2,340 square feet
Second Floor: 1,806 square feet
Total: 4,146 square feet

Finished Basement: 1,608 square feet
Bonus Space: 442 square feet
Width: 117'-6" Depth: 74'-5"

DESIGN HPT880126

Vaulted Great Room

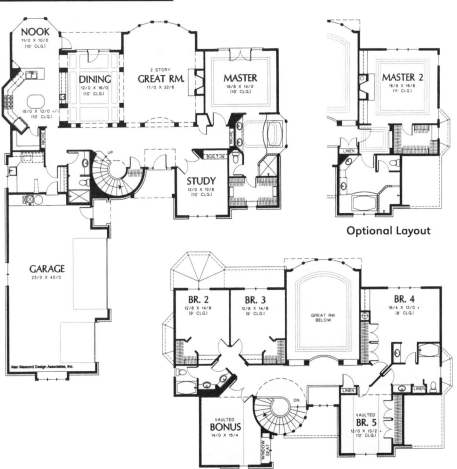

Optional Layout

Alan Mascord Design Associates, Inc.

With sturdy brick detailing, sweeping rooflines and a turret that settles seamlessly into the facade, this fine five-bedroom home will be a winner in any neighborhood. Inside, the two-story foyer leads directly to the spacious great room. A study hides to the right of the foyer, offering privacy. The formal dining room is graced with a ten-foot ceiling, a pass-through to the kitchen and direct access to the backyard. The C-shaped kitchen features a six-burner stove, work island, lage walk-in pantry and a nearby octagonal nook. The lavish master suite offers two floor plans—the smaller version presents a walk-in closet and a bath with separate tub and shower, while the larger option includes a fireplace and a much larger bath (in place of the study).

First Floor: 2,356 square feet
Second Floor: 1,450 square feet
Total: 3,806 square feet

Bonus Space: 261 square feet
Width: 67'-0" Depth: 82'-0"

Decorative Stickwork

Keystone arches, a wonderful turret, vertical shutters and decorative stickwork over the entry add to the charm of this fine home. A formal dining room at the front of the plan is complemented by the breakfast bay at the rear. An angled snack bar/counter separates the island kitchen from the gathering room.

An adjoining recreation room offers a wet bar and a second flight of stairs to the sleeping quarters. Bay windows brighten the master suite and Suite 2, both with private baths. Two more bedrooms share a full bath that includes a dressing area and twin vanities. The laundry room is on this level for convenience.

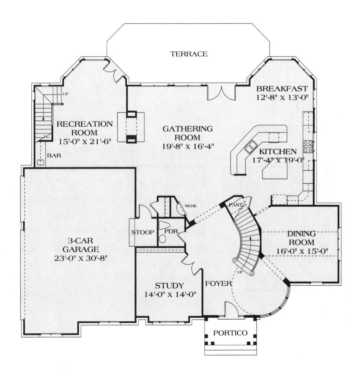

First Floor: 2,267 square feet
Second Floor: 2,209 square feet
Total: 4,476 square feet

Width: 67'-2" Depth: 64'-10"

DESIGN HPT880128

Recreation Room

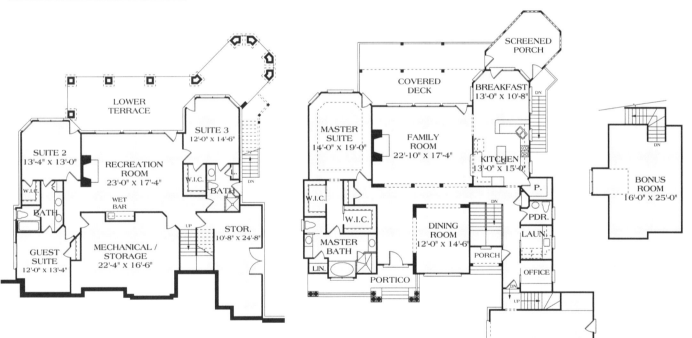

LOWER TERRACE

SUITE 3
12'-0" x 14'-6"

SUITE 2
13'-4" x 13'-0"

RECREATION ROOM
23'-0" x 17'-4"

W.I.C.

BATH

W.I.C.

BATH

WET BAR

STOR.
10'-8" x 24'-8"

GUEST SUITE
12'-0" x 13'-4"

MECHANICAL / STORAGE
22'-4" x 16'-6"

MASTER SUITE
14'-0" x 19'-0"

COVERED DECK

SCREENED PORCH

BREAKFAST
13'-0" x 10'-8"

FAMILY ROOM
22'-10" x 17'-4"

KITCHEN
13'-0" x 15'-0"

W.I.C.

W.I.C.

P.

PDR.

DINING ROOM
12'-0" x 14'-6"

MASTER BATH

LIN.

PORTICO

PORCH

LAUN.

OFFICE

GARAGE
23'-4" x 23'-6"

BONUS ROOM
16'-0" x 25'-0"

Interesting window treatments highlight this stone-and-shake facade, but don't overlook the columned porch to the left of the portico. Arches outline the formal dining room and the family room, both of which are convenient to the island kitchen. Household chores are made easier by the placement of a pantry, powder room, laundry room and office between the kitchen and the entrances to the side porch and garage. If your goal is relaxation, the breakfast room, screened porch and covered deck are also nearby. The master suite features a beautiful bay, while three secondary bedrooms and a recreation room are on the lower level.

Main Level: 2,213 square feet
Lower Level: 1,333 square feet
Total: 3,546 square feet

Bonus Room: 430 square feet
Width: 67'-2" Depth: 93'-1"

Attractive Stone Exterior

Gently flaring eaves and curved dormers contrast with the straight rooflines and angled gables on this attractive stone exterior. A breezeway connects the house to the three-car garage, above which an apartment offers living space for a mother-in-law or grown child. On the second floor of the main house, you'll find three more bedroom suites, a sewing room and a future exercise room. Downstairs, the foyer opens to the formal dining room and leads ahead to the grand room, elegant and inviting with its massive fireplace, built-ins and French doors to the terrace. A large informal area features a second fireplace and includes a gathering room, a breakfast nook and an island kitchen with a huge walk-in pantry. Amenities in the master suite include two walk-in closets, a corner garden tub and dual vanities. A wet bar is shared with the nearby study, which boasts a third fireplace.

First Floor: 3,347 square feet
Second Floor: 1,696 square feet
Total: 5,043 square feet

Apartment: 714 square feet
Width: 120'-0" Depth: 99'-11"

DESIGN HPT880130

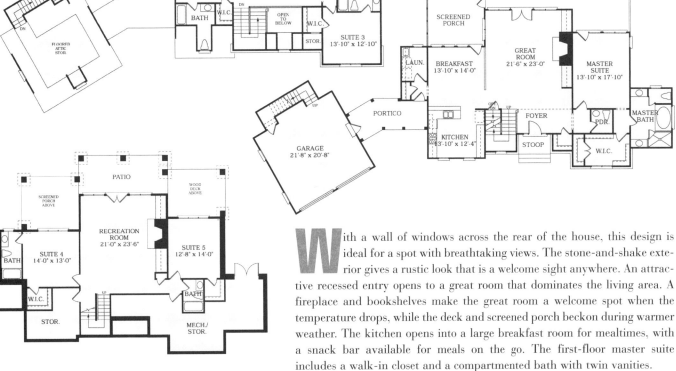

SUITE 4 / LOFT
14'-0" x 19'-0"

BALCONY

BATH

W.I.C.

OPEN TO BELOW

OPEN TO BELOW

W.I.C.

STOR.

SUITE 2
13'-10" x 11'-0"

BATH

SUITE 3
13'-10" x 12'-10"

FLOORED ATTIC STOR.

DECK

SCREENED PORCH

GREAT ROOM
21'-6" x 23'-0"

MASTER SUITE
13'-10" x 17'-10"

LAUN.

BREAKFAST
13'-10" x 14'-0"

PORTICO

GARAGE
21'-8" x 20'-8"

KITCHEN
13'-10" x 12'-4"

FOYER

STOOP

PDR.

MASTER BATH

W.I.C.

PATIO

WOOD DECK ABOVE

SCREENED PORCH ABOVE

RECREATION ROOM
21'-0" x 23'-6"

SUITE 5
12'-8" x 14'-0"

SUITE 4
14'-0" x 13'-0"

BATH

W.I.C.

STOR.

BATH

MECH./ STOR.

With a wall of windows across the rear of the house, this design is ideal for a spot with breathtaking views. The stone-and-shake exterior gives a rustic look that is a welcome sight anywhere. An attractive recessed entry opens to a great room that dominates the living area. A fireplace and bookshelves make the great room a welcome spot when the temperature drops, while the deck and screened porch beckon during warmer weather. The kitchen opens into a large breakfast room for mealtimes, with a snack bar available for meals on the go. The first-floor master suite includes a walk-in closet and a compartmented bath with twin vanities.

First Floor: 1,793 square feet
Second Floor: 1,115 square feet
Total: 2,908 square feet

Finished Basement: 915 square feet
Width: 103'-8" **Depth:** 57'-6"

A Quiet Getaway

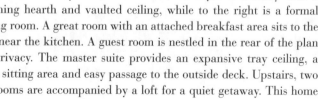

Cost to build? See page 214
to order complete cost estimate
to build this house in your area!

The striking combination of wood framing, shingles and glass creates the exterior of this classic cottage. The foyer opens to the main-level layout. To the left of the foyer is a study with a warming hearth and vaulted ceiling, while to the right is a formal dining room. A great room with an attached breakfast area sits to the rear near the kitchen. A guest room is nestled in the rear of the plan for privacy. The master suite provides an expansive tray ceiling, a glass sitting area and easy passage to the outside deck. Upstairs, two bedrooms are accompanied by a loft for a quiet getaway. This home is designed with a walkout basement foundation.

First Floor: 2,070 square feet
Second Floor: 790 square feet
Total: 2,860 square feet

Width: 58'-4" Depth: 54'-10"

DESIGN HPT880132

Secluded Den with Built-ins

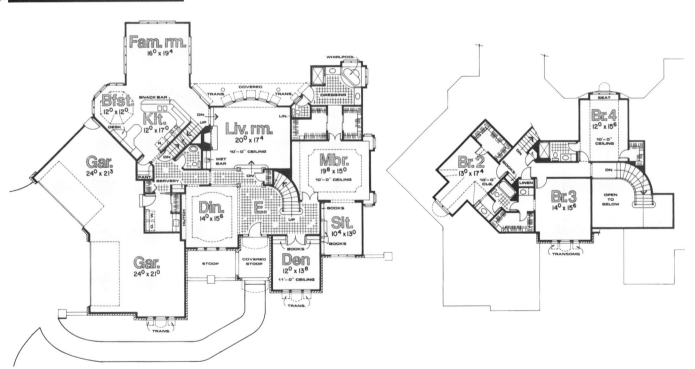

Keystone lintels, an arched transom over the entry and sidelights spell classic design for this four-bedroom home. The tiled foyer offers entry to any room you choose, whether it be the secluded den with its built-in bookshelves, the formal dining room, the formal living room with its fireplace, wet bar and wall of windows, or the spacious rear family and kitchen area with its sunny breakfast nook. The master suite offers privacy on the first floor and features a sitting room with bookshelves, two walk-in closets and a private bath with a corner whirlpool tub. Upstairs, two family bedrooms share a bath and enjoy separate vanities. A third family bedroom features its own full bath and a built-in window seat in a box-bay window.

First Floor: 2,813 square feet
Second Floor: 1,091 square feet
Total: 3,904 square feet

Width: 85'-5" Depth: 74'-8"

Entertainment Terrace

© Copyright 2002, The Sater Design Collection, Inc.

Bedroom 2
13'-0" x 12'-0"
9'-4" Clg.

Open to Below
21'-0" to 21'-8"
Coffered Clg.

Bonus Room
13'-8" x 14'-0"
Vault to 9'-10" Clg.

WIC

Dn

WIC

Bath 1
9'-0" Clg.

Walk-In Shower

Niche

Walk-In Shower

WIC

Bonus Bath
8'-0" Clg.

Walk-In Shower

Bath 2
9'-0" Clg.

Computer Loft
9'-0" Clg.

WIC

Dn

Desk

Bedroom 1
13'-0" x 12'-6"
12'-0" Clg.

Guest Suite
13'-0" x 11'-8"
9'-0" Clg.

Deck

© Copyright 2002, The Sater Design Collection, Inc.

Veranda
15'-4" Clg.

Breakfast
9'-4" to 10'-0"
Beamed Clg.

Outdoor Grille

Built-Ins

Kitchen
14'-6" x 10'-6"
9'-4" to 10'-0"
Beamed Clg.

Master Suite
17'-0" x 14'-8"
12'-0" to 13'-0"
Tray Clg.

WIC

Great Room
21'-0" x 17'-0"
Open to Above

Fireplace

Dn

Up

Garage
24'-0" x 23'-0"
10'-2" Clg.

Entertainment Center

Storage

Art Niche

Master Bath
12'-0" Clg.

Whirlpool

Up

Foyer
9'-4" to 10'-0"
Stepped Clg.

Dining
13'-0" x 13'-0"
9'-0" to 10'-0"
Stepped Clg.

Pantry
8'-8" Clg.

Utility
8'-0" Clg.

Walk-In Shower

Powder Bath
11'-0" Clg.

Study/Office
13'-8" x 13'-0"
9'-4" to 10'-0"
Beamed Clg.

Portico
11'-0" Clg.

Stucco and stone combine with graceful details on this four-bedroom home. A covered front porch welcomes friends and family alike, and ushers you into the elegant foyer. A formal dining room is to your right, defined by columns and a grand ceiling treatment. Convenient to the front door as well as to the lavish master suite, a study/office provides a bay window and lots of privacy. The spacious great room offers a warming fireplace, built-ins and a pass-through to the efficient kitchen. Here, the gourmet of the family will be well pleased with a worktop island, plenty of wrapping counters and a huge pantry nearby. Separated on the first floor for privacy, the master suite is full of tempting amenities.

First Floor: 2,222 square feet
Second Floor: 1,075 square feet
Total: 3,297 square feet

Bonus Space: 405 square feet
Width: 91'-0" Depth: 52'-8"

DESIGN HPT880134

Flex Space

This English manor is sure to please, with its attractive facade and accommodating interior. The wraparound portico leads to the graceful foyer. Here, a formal dining room opens to the right and offers a refined ceiling treatment, while the study/office is to the left and features a bay window. The spacious great room provides a fireplace, built-ins, an entertainment center and access to the rear veranda. The sumptuous kitchen provides a worktop island, a beamed ceiling and a nearby bayed breakfast nook. The lavish first-floor master suite is complete with a large, skylit walk-in closet, deluxe bath and private access to the rear veranda. Upstairs, a computer loft separates the guest suite from the family bedrooms.

First Floor: 2,222 square feet
Second Floor: 1,075 square feet
Total: 3,297 square feet

Bonus Space: 405 square feet
Width: 91'-0" Depth: 52'-8"

Graceful Rooflines

Elegant details on this four-bedroom home include a trio of dormers, an attractive bay window and graceful rooflines. Inside, the two-story foyer presents the formal living room, complete with a warming fireplace, a bay window and a vaulted ceiling. The formal dining room opens directly off this room, and offers easy access to the spacious island kitchen via a butler's pantry. The family room features a built-in media center and shares a fireplace with the cozy den. A wet bar is conveniently located between the family room, kitchen and dining room. Up the curved staircase, three family bedrooms share a hall bath with twin vanities. A large game room provides built-in storage and privacy for the children. The master suite is full of amenities, including a huge walk-in closet, separate tub and shower, twin vanities and a vaulted ceiling.

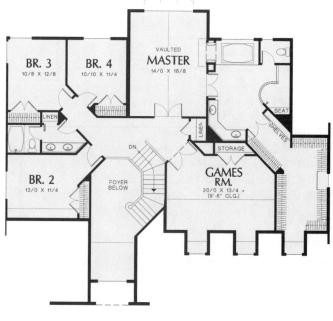

First Floor: 1,998 square feet
Second Floor: 1,898 square feet
Total: 3,896 square feet

Width: 60'-0" Depth: 56'-4"

English
Cottages

To view floor plans, see page 29.

Built-in Media Center

Second Floor Plan:

BONUS RM.
21/0 X 18/0 +/-
(9' CLG.)

MASTER BR.
17/0 X 19/2
(10' CLG.)

BR. 2
11/4 X 14/10
(9' CLG.)

DN.

LINEN

BR. 4
12/0 X 13/2
(9' CLG.)

LINEN

DN.

FOYER
BELOW

BR. 3
12/0 X 13/10 +
(9' CLG.)

PLANT
SHELF

First Floor Plan:

© Alan Mascord Design Associates, Inc.

NOOK
11/0 X 12/0
(10' CLG.)

MEDIA
CENTER

FAMILY RM.
22/0 X 18/6 +/-
(10' CLG.)

KITCHEN
12/0 X 19/2
(10' CLG.)

REF.

BUILT-IN

DINING RM.
12/0 X 15/0
(13'-6" CLG.)

BUTLER'S
PANTRY

DESK

O.

GARAGE
22/0 X 33/0 +
(10' CLG.)

UP

SH.   SH.

STOR.

TWO STORY
FOYER
15/2 X 11/6 +/-

D. W.

STUDY
12/0 X 16/2
(10' CLG.)

UP

LIVING RM.
15/0 X 18/6
(14'-1" CLG.)

Shingles, stone and shutters all combine to give this attractive manor a warm and welcoming feel. The two-story foyer presents the formal living room on the right—complete with a fireplace. The spacious family room also features a fireplace, along with a built-in media center, a wall of windows and a ten-foot ceiling. Open to the family room, the efficient kitchen provides plenty of cabinet and counter space, as well as a nearby bayed nook. A study with built-in bookshelves opens from the central gallery hall. Upstairs, the master suite includes a walk-in closet, a pampering bath with dual vanities and a tub set in a bay, a ten-foot ceiling and a corner fireplace.

First Floor: 2,451 square feet
Second Floor: 2,115 square feet
Total: 4,566 square feet

Bonus Room: 353 square feet
Width: 92'-6"   Depth: 46'-0"

DESIGN HPT880138

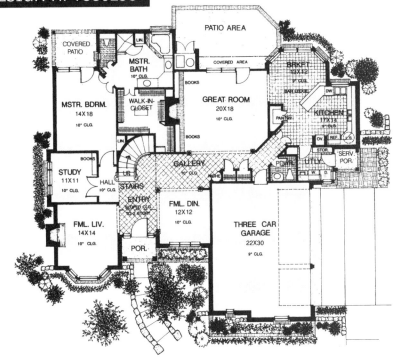

Here's a cottage that would have provided plenty of room for Goldilocks AND the three bears! Wonderful rooflines top a brick exterior with cedar and stone accents—and lots of English country charm. Stone wing walls extend the front profile, and a cedar hood tops the large bay window. The two-story entry reveals a graceful curving staircase and opens to the formal living and dining rooms. Fireplaces are found in the living room as well as the great room, which also boasts built-in bookcases and access to the rear patio. The kitchen and breakfast room add to the informal area and include a snack bar. A private patio is part of the master suite, which also offers an intriguing corner tub, twin vanities, a large walk-in closet and a nearby study. Three family bedrooms and a bonus room comprise the second floor.

First Floor: 2,438 square feet
Second Floor: 882 square feet
Total: 3,320 square feet

Bonus Space: 230 square feet
Width: 70'-0" Depth: 63'-2"

Charming Country Flavor

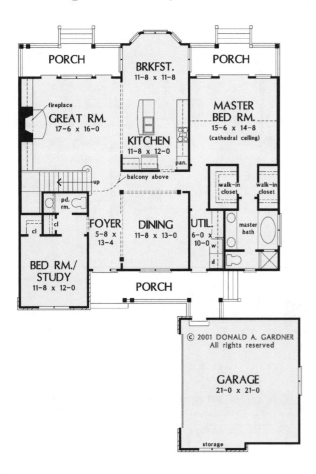

PORCH

BRKFST.
11-8 x 11-8

PORCH

fireplace

GREAT RM.
17-6 x 16-0

MASTER
BED RM.
15-6 x 14-8
(cathedral ceiling)

KITCHEN
11-8 x 12-0

pan.

balcony above

up

walk-in
closet

walk-in
closet

pd.
rm.

cl

cl

FOYER
5-8 x
13-4

DINING
11-8 x 13-0

UTIL.
6-0 x
10-0

master
bath

w

d

BED RM./
STUDY
11-8 x 12-0

PORCH

GARAGE
21-0 x 21-0

storage

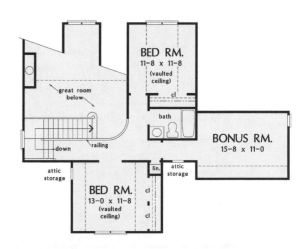

great room
below

BED RM.
11-8 x 11-8
(vaulted ceiling)

cl

bath

down

railing

BONUS RM.
15-8 x 11-0

attic
storage

BED RM.
13-0 x 11-8
(vaulted ceiling)

cl

cl

lin.

cl

attic
storage

Gable treatments along with stone and horizontal siding give a definite country flavor to this two-story home. The front study makes an ideal guest room with the adjoining powder room. The formal dining room is accented with decorative columns that define its perimeter. The great room boasts a fireplace, built-ins and a magnificent view of the backyard beyond one of two rear porches. The master suite boasts two walk-in closets and a private bath. Two bedrooms share a full bath on the second floor.

First Floor: 1,707 square feet
Second Floor: 514 square feet
Total: 2,221 square feet

Bonus Room: 211 square feet
Width: 50'-0" Depth: 71'-8"

DESIGN HPT880140

Plush Retreat

DECK

TWO STORY
GREAT ROOM
14'-0" X 18'-0"

BREAKFAST
10'-0" X 10'-0"

KITCHEN
12'-6" X 11'-0"

MEDIA ROOM
12'-0" X 15'-6"

UP

LAUNDRY

POWDER

DN

DINING ROOM
12'-0" X 11'-6"

UP

TWO STORY
FOYER
10'-6" X 10'-8"

LIVING ROOM
13'-4" X 10'-6"

TWO CAR GARAGE
21'-10" X 22'-0"

STOOP

BEDROOM NO. 2
12'-0" X 12'-0"

OPEN TO BELOW

SITTING

MASTER BEDROOM
19'-8" X 13'-6"

BALCONY

W.I.C.

W.I.C.

BATH

DN

MASTER
BATH

BEDROOM NO. 3
12'-0" X 12'-6"

OPEN TO
BELOW

W.I.C.

UNFIN. BONUS
12'-0" X 11'-4"

QUOTE ONE®
Cost to build? See page 214
to order complete cost estimate
to build this house in your area!

The well-balanced use of stucco and stone combined with box-bay window treatments and a covered entry make this English country home especially inviting. The two-story foyer opens on the right to formal living and dining rooms, bright with natural light. A spacious U-shaped kitchen adjoins a breakfast nook with views of the outdoors. This area flows nicely into the two-story great room, which offers a through-fireplace to the media room. A plush retreat awaits the homeowner upstairs with a master suite that offers a quiet, windowed sitting area with views to the rear grounds. Two family bedrooms share a full bath and a balcony hall that has a dramatic view of the great room below. This home is designed with a basement foundation.

First Floor: 1,395 square feet
Second Floor: 1,210 square feet
Total: 2,605 square feet

Bonus Space: 225 square feet
Width: 47'-0" Depth: 49'-6"

Convenient Dressing Area

Handsome detailing and unique windows are hallmarks on the elevation of this two-story design. Triple-arch windows in the front and rear of the great room create an impressive view. Counter space is coordinated in the island kitchen to make it easy to prepare meals. The left wing of the plan is dedicated to the lavish master suite, which boasts a walk-in closet. The compartmented bath provides a convenient dressing area and vanity space. In the entry, a U-shaped staircase with a window leads to a second-floor balcony, two bedrooms and a full bath.

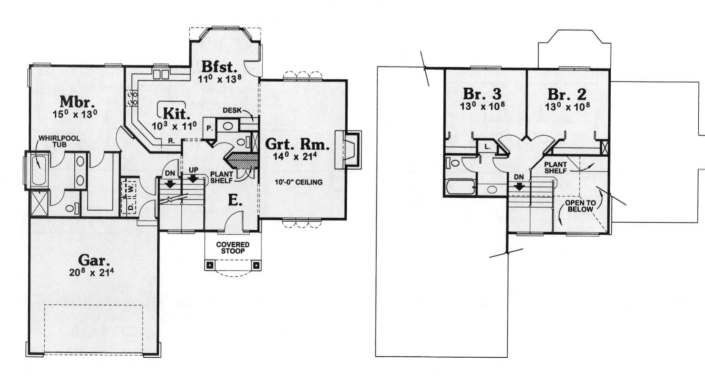

First Floor: 1,314 square feet
Second Floor: 458 square feet
Total: 1,772 square feet

Width: 52'-0" Depth: 51'-4"

DESIGN HPT880142

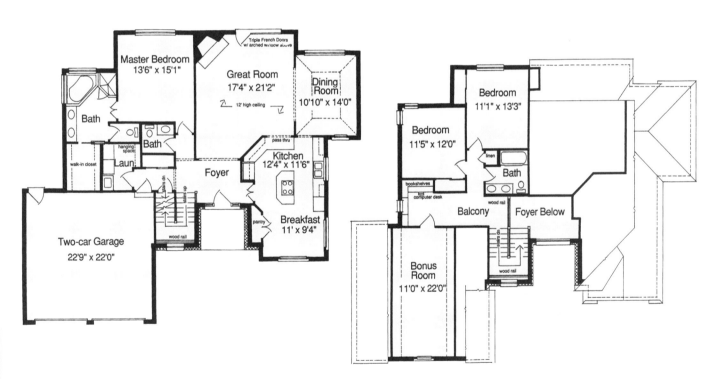

Master Bedroom 13'6" x 15'1"

Great Room 17'4" x 21'2"

12' high ceiling

Triple French Doors w/ arched window above

Dining Room 10'10" x 14'0"

Bath

Bath

hanging space

walk-in closet

Laun.

pass thru

Foyer

Kitchen 12'4" x 11'6"

Two-car Garage 22'9" x 22'0"

stairs dn stairs up

wood rail

pantry

Breakfast 11' x 9'4"

Bedroom 11'1" x 13'3"

Bedroom 11'5" x 12'0"

linen

bookshelves

computer desk

Bath

wood rail

Balcony

Foyer Below

stairs dn

wood rail

Bonus Room 11'0" x 22'0"

An interesting roofline and multi-textured exterior provide a rich, solid look to this extraordinary home. From the foyer, your view will go directly to the cozy fireplace and stylish French doors of the great room. A grand entry into the formal dining room, coupled with the volume ceiling, pulls these two rooms together for a spacious feeling. Natural light floods the breakfast area making this a bright and cheery place to start your day. Split stairs lead to the second floor where a balcony overlooking the foyer directs you to two secluded bedrooms or to a computer area with a desk and bookshelves.

First Floor: 1,524 square feet
Second Floor: 558 square feet
Total: 2,082 square feet

Bonus Room: 267 square feet
Width: 60'-0" Depth: 50'-4"

© 1997 Donald A Gardner Architects, Inc.

Great Master Suite

There's not a bit of wasted space in this cozy, well-designed home. Sunburst windows decorate the exterior and fill the interior with light. Double columns lend elegance to the foyer, which opens to a spacious great room with a cathedral ceiling, a fireplace and access to the rear porch. The formal dining room features a bay window that offers wide views of the property. Split sleeping quarters include a master suite with a walk-in closet, oversized shower and garden tub, as well as two secondary bedrooms that share a full bath.

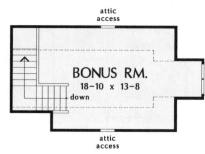

attic access

BONUS RM.
18-10 x 13-8
down

attic access

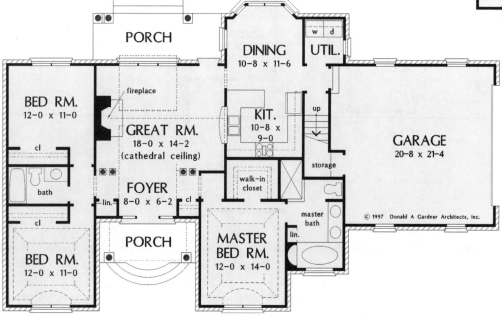

© 1997 Donald A Gardner Architects, Inc.

Square Footage: 1,488
Bonus Room: 338 square feet

Width: 69'-7" Depth: 42'-0"

B. NATHAN · © 1997 Donald A. Gardner Architects, Inc.

DESIGN HPT880144

Wrapped in Windows

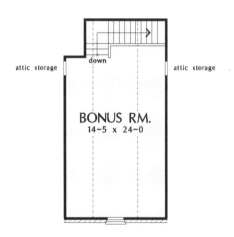

PORCH

DINING
11-4 x 12-0

(dormers above)

PORCH

master bath

walk-in closet   walk-in closet

UTIL.
7-0 x 10-0

KIT.
13-0 x 12-0

shelves

fireplace

MASTER BED RM.
13-0 x 14-8

pan.

(cathedral ceiling)

storage

GREAT RM.
17-8 x 20-4

up

cl

cl   lin.

GARAGE
22-0 x 24-0

FOYER
8-0 x 7-3

bath

BED RM.
11-4 x 11-8

PORCH

© 1997 Donald A Gardner Architects, Inc.

BED RM.
11-0 x 11-0

attic storage   down   attic storage

BONUS RM.
14-5 x 24-0

Similar elements are arranged asymmetrically to add interest to this brick cottage's exterior. Keystone arches and shutters accent small-pane windows. The floor plan is simple and practical. The great room, the heart of the home, includes a focal-point fireplace, built-in shelves, a cathedral ceiling and access to a rear covered porch. The bumped-out dining room is elegant, octagonal in shape and wrapped in windows to enhance mealtimes with natural sunlight or moonlight. A second porch leads into a sizable utility room off the kitchen.

Square Footage: 1,829
Bonus Room: 424 square feet

Width: 54'-11" Depth: 58'-7"

Great Outdoor Spaces

PATIO

PORCH

SITTING
9–10 x 4–6

MASTER
BED RM.
14–0 x 15–0

BRKFST.
14–8 x 13–2

(cathedral ceiling)

GREAT RM.
15–8 x 21–10

BED RM.
12–4 x 11–0

cl

lin.

bath

KITCHEN
14–8 x 10–0

pan.

UTIL.
6–0 x
9–8

w
d

master
bath

lin.

walk–in
closet

fireplace

walk–in
closet

cl

up

sto.

FOYER
8–0 x
8–8

DINING
12–4 x 13–0

GARAGE
22–0 x 23–0

BED RM./
STUDY
12–4 x 11–4

PORCH

storage

© 1996 Donald A. Gardner Architects, Inc.

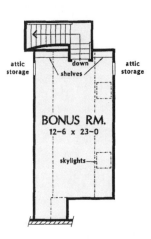

attic
storage

down
shelves

attic
storage

BONUS RM.
12–6 x 23–0

skylights

This plan's stunning brick-and-siding exterior surrounds well-planned living spaces to create a home where formal gatherings or casual family moments are equal pleasures. The heart of this comfortably elegant home is the great room, which opens to the breakfast area, the formal dining room and the foyer. Bay windows in the breakfast area and the master bedroom echo one another to provide a great master sitting area and a dramatic rear elevation. The master suite is also equipped with a spacious, pampering bath with a corner shower, a garden tub, an enclosed toilet and a sizable walk-in closet.

Square Footage: 2,196
Bonus Room: 326 square feet

Width: 64'-4"   Depth: 66'-4"

DESIGN HPT880146

Comfort and Tradition

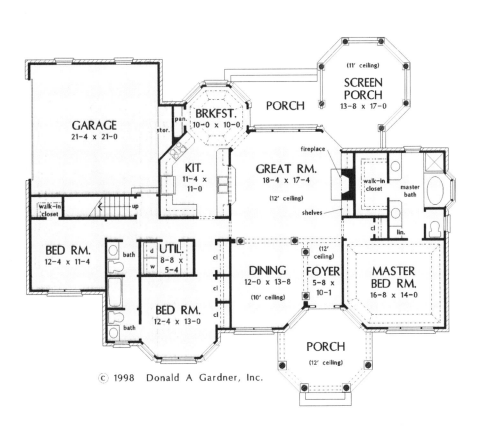

© 1998 Donald A Gardner, Inc.

GARAGE
21-4 x 21-0

BRKFST.
10-0 x 10-0

PORCH

SCREEN
PORCH
13-8 x 17-0
(11' ceiling)

pan.

stor.

KIT.
11-4 x
11-0

GREAT RM.
18-4 x 17-4
(12' ceiling)

fireplace

walk-in
closet

master
bath

shelves

cl

lin.

walk-in
closet

BED RM.
12-4 x 11-4

bath

d UTIL
8-8 x
w 5-4

cl

DINING
12-0 x 13-8
(10' ceiling)

FOYER
5-8 x
10-1

(12'
ceiling)

MASTER
BED RM.
16-8 x 14-0

up

cl

BED RM.
12-4 x 13-0

cl

bath

PORCH
(12' ceiling)

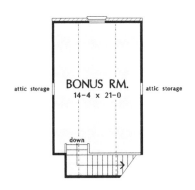

BONUS RM.
14-4 x 21-0

attic storage

attic storage

down

An octagonal front porch complements a spacious outdoor area to
the rear of this plan—which
boasts a screened porch. Inside, an
octagonal breakfast room and a bay-
windowed bedroom enhance this open
plan, designed with a perfect balance of
comfort and tradition. Columns, turrets
and unusual windows add interest. The
foyer connects through columns with
the dining room and the great room.
Separated from family bedrooms for
privacy, the master suite provides a
great retreat. Two family bedrooms
share a bath but have separate dressing
areas, each with a vanity and a toilet.

Square Footage: 2,014
Bonus Room: 377 square feet

Width: 71'-5" Depth: 57'-6"

Twin Walk-in Closets

The open-plan living areas of this design are perfect for the modern family with a taste for classic design. The exterior is traditional brick accentuated with corner quoins and graceful arched windows. A formal dining room and study—or optional bedroom—flank the entry foyer, which leads to the great room. The expanse of the great room is heightened with a ten-foot ceiling, and a welcoming fireplace adds warmth. A gourmet kitchen with breakfast island opens to a bayed breakfast nook overlooking a covered porch and patio. A master bedroom features a whirlpool tub recessed between twin walk-in closets. Two family bedrooms share a full bath to complete the plan. Please specify basement, crawlspace or slab foundation when ordering.

Square Footage: 2,107

Width: 64'-8" Depth: 62'-0"

DESIGN HPT880148

Charming Tudor

Quote One®
Cost to build? See page 214
to order complete cost estimate
to build this house in your area!

Just the right amount of living space is contained in this charming traditional Tudor house and it is arranged in a great floor plan. The split-bedroom configuration, with two bedrooms (or optional study) on the first floor and the master suite on the second floor with its own studio, assures complete privacy. The living room has a second-floor balcony overlook and a warming fireplace. The full-width terrace in back is reached through sliding glass doors in each room at the rear of the house.

First Floor: 1,467 square feet
Second Floor: 715 square feet
Total: 2,182 square feet

Width: 55'-8" Depth: 55'-0"

L

Optional Bonus Room

A careful blend of siding and stone lends eye-catching appeal to this traditional plan. Vaulted ceilings grace the great room, master bath and dining room. The master suite features a tray ceiling and a deluxe private bath. A bedroom/study is located on the first floor. Two second-floor bedrooms easily access a full bath. An optional bonus room offers plenty of room to grow—making it perfect for a guest suite, home office or exercise room. Please specify basement or crawlspace foundation when ordering.

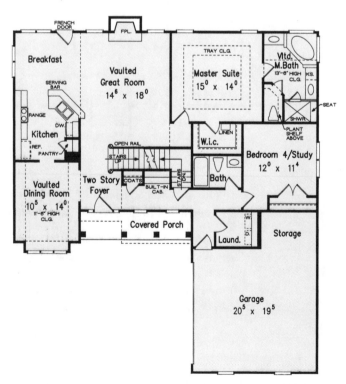

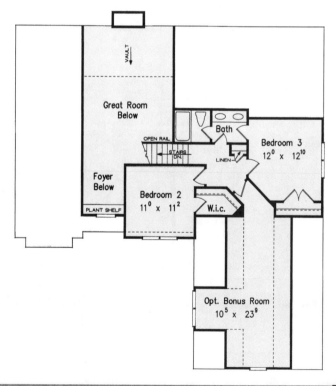

First Floor: 1,559 square feet
Second Floor: 475 square feet
Total: 2,034 square feet

Bonus Space: 321 square feet
Width: 50'-0" Depth: 56'-4"

DESIGN HPT880150

Magnificent Master Suite

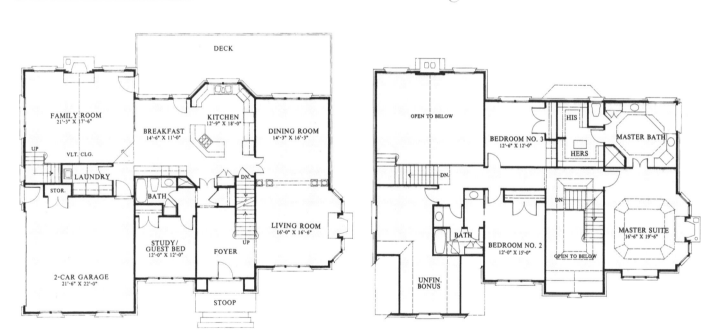

DECK

FAMILY ROOM
21'-3" X 17'-6"

KITCHEN
12'-9" X 18'-0"

BREAKFAST
14'-6" X 11'-0"

DINING ROOM
14'-3" X 16'-3"

UP

VLT. CLG.

LAUNDRY

STOR.

BATH

DN

LIVING ROOM
16'-0" X 16'-6"

STUDY/
GUEST BED
12'-0" X 12'-0"

FOYER

UP

2-CAR GARAGE
21'-6" X 22'-0"

STOOP

OPEN TO BELOW

HIS

BEDROOM NO. 3
12'-6" X 12'-0"

MASTER BATH

HERS

DN.

DN.

BATH

BEDROOM NO. 2
12'-0" X 15'-0"

OPEN TO BELOW

MASTER SUITE
16'-6" X 19'-6"

UNFIN.
BONUS

This English manor features a dramatic brick exterior, highlighted with a varied roofline and a finial atop the uppermost gable. The main level opens to a two-story foyer, with the formal rooms on the right. The living room contains a fireplace set in a bay window. The dining room is separated from the living room by a symmetrical column arrangement. The more casual family room is to the rear. For guests, a bedroom and bath are located on the main level. The second floor provides additional bedrooms and baths for family as well as a magnificent master suite. This home is designed with a walkout basement foundation.

QUOTE ONE®
Cost to build? See page 214
to order complete cost estimate
to build this house in your area!

First Floor: 1,847 square feet
Second Floor: 1,453 square feet
Total: 3,300 square feet

Width: 63'-3" Depth: 47'-0"

European Details

Interesting angles and creative detailing characterize the exterior of this brick cottage. Inside, the formal dining room is just off the foyer for ease in entertaining. A gallery hall leads to the island kitchen, which opens to an informal dining area with access to two covered patios. Sleeping quarters include two family bedrooms to the right of the plan and another bedroom, which could be used as a study, on the left. The left wing is dedicated to a lavish master suite complete with a vaulted ceiling and sumptuous bath with a whirlpool tub and separate shower.

Square Footage: 2,526

Width: 64'-0" Depth: 81'-7"

DESIGN HPT880152

English-Timbered Ceiling

With a wonderfully quaint appearance, this fine English manor has tons to offer. Inside to the right of the foyer, a formal dining room awaits, accented by a timbered ceiling and offering a dining terrace covered by an oak trellis. An efficient kitchen is nearby. The spacious great room is complete with a fireplace, a multitude of windows and is open up to the rafter beams. Separated for privacy, the first-floor master suite includes a walk-in closet, a lavish bath, a sitting alcove, direct access to the rear terrace and an English-timbered ceiling. Upstairs, two large bedrooms provide plenty of storage and share a hall bath.

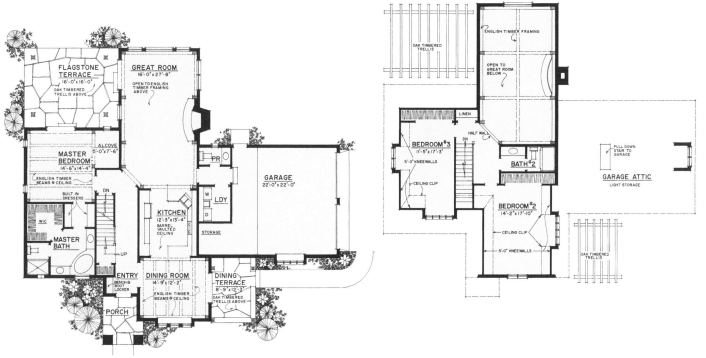

First Floor: 1,668 square feet
Second Floor: 782 square feet
Total: 2,450 square feet

Width: 67'-2" Depth: 60'-0"

Delightful Layout

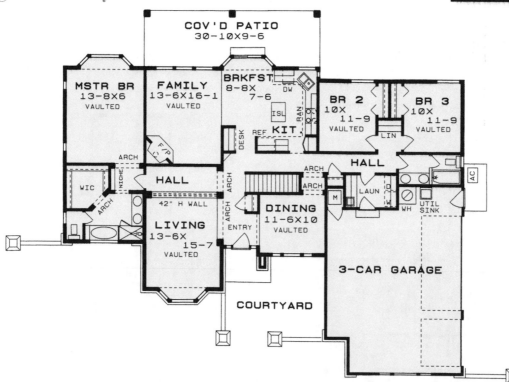

COV'D PATIO
30-10X9-6

MSTR BR
13-8X6
VAULTED

FAMILY
13-6X16-1
VAULTED

BRKFST
8-8X
7-6

BR 2
10X
11-9
VAULTED

BR 3
10X
11-9
VAULTED

ISL

DW

RAN

KIT

REF

DESK

WIC

ARCH

NICHE

FIR

ARCH

HALL
42" H WALL

LIVING
13-6X
15-7
VAULTED

ARCH
ARCH

ENTRY

DINING
11-6X10
VAULTED

ARCH

ARCH

HALL

LIN

LAUN

M

D

W

WH

UTIL
SINK

AC

COURTYARD

3-CAR GARAGE

This cute one-story English home may seem small, but it's full of amenities. A formal dining room is to the right of the foyer, while a formal living room on the left offers a bay window and a vaulted ceiling. The family room features a corner fireplace, wall of windows and easy access to the bayed breakfast nook and the efficient kitchen. Here, a work island, built-in desk and corner window sink highlight a delightful layout. Two family bedrooms share a hall bath and are convenient to the laundry room. Separated for privacy, the master suite is complete with a large walk-in closet, a bay window and a lavish bath.

Square Footage: 2,050

Width: 70'0" Depth: 61'-6"

Designs from the Mediterranean

To view floor plans, see page 12.

A Dream Come True

verandah

leisure
17'-0" x 18'-4"
10' flat ceiling

nook
10'-0" x 10'-0"
10' flat clg.

wet bar

lanai

master suite
15'-8" x 15'-0"
11' flat clg.

verandah
24'-0" x 11'-0"

grill

kitchen
12' x 16'

br. 2
11'-8" x 13'-4"
10' flat clg.

private garden

his

hers

living room
14'-8" x 14'-8" avg.
14' flat ceiling

dining
14'-8" x 14'-8" avg.
14' flat clg.

art niche

arch

utility

br. 3
14'-0" x 11'-4"
10' flat clg.

gallery foyer

art niche

entry porch

study
11'-4" x 13'-4"
10' flat clg.

garage
22'-8" x 28'-0"

This home is designed to be a homeowner's dream come true. A formal living area opens from the gallery foyer through graceful arches and looks out to the veranda, which hosts an outdoor grill and service counter, perfect for outdoor entertaining. The leisure room offers a private veranda, a cabana bath and a wet bar just off the gourmet kitchen. Walls of windows and a bayed breakfast nook let in natural light and set a bright tone for this area. The master suite opens to the rear property through French doors, and boasts a lavish bath with a corner whirlpool tub that overlooks a private garden. An art niche off the gallery hall, a private dressing area and a secluded study complement the master suite.

Square Footage: 2,978

Width: 84'-0" Depth: 90'-0"

© 1994 Donald A. Gardner Architects, Inc.

B. NATHAN

DESIGN HPT880156

Winning Combination

Arched windows and a dramatic arched entry enhance this exciting contemporary home. The expansive great room, highlighted by a cathedral ceiling and a fireplace, offers direct access to the rear patio and the formal dining room—a winning combination for both formal and informal get-togethers. An efficient U-shaped kitchen provides plenty of counter space and easily serves both the dining room and the great room. Sunlight fills the master bedroom through a wall of windows, which affords views of the rear grounds. The master bath invites relaxation with its soothing corner tub and separate shower. Two secondary bedrooms—one serves as an optional study—share an adjacent bath.

© 1994 Donald A. Gardner Architects, Inc.

Square Footage: 1,838   Width: 60'-0" Depth: 60'-4"

Wealth of Livability

Direct from the Mediterranean, this Spanish-style, one-story home offers a practical floor plan. The facade features arch-top, multi-pane windows, a columned front porch, a tall chimney and a tiled roof. The interior has a wealth of livability. What you'll appreciate first is the juxtaposition of the great room and the formal dining room—both defined by columns. A more casual eating area is attached to the L-shaped kitchen and accesses a screened porch, as does the great room. Three bedrooms mean abundant sleeping space. The study could be a fourth bedroom—choose the full bath option in this case. A tray ceiling decorates the master suite, which is further enhanced by a bath with a separate shower and tub, walk-in closet and double sinks.

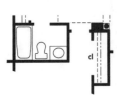

(optional full bath)

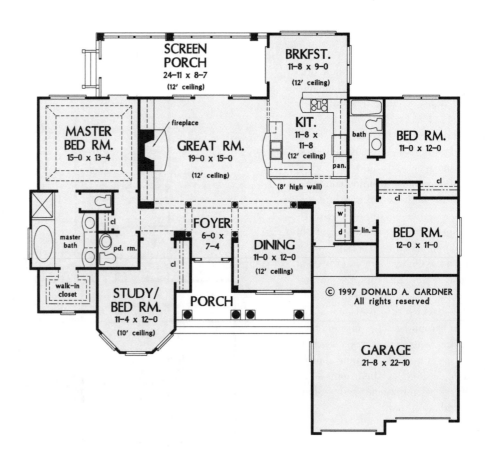

SCREEN PORCH
24–11 x 8–7
(12' ceiling)

BRKFST.
11–8 x 9–0
(12' ceiling)

MASTER BED RM.
15–0 x 13–4

fireplace

GREAT RM.
19–0 x 15–0
(12' ceiling)

KIT.
11–8 x 11–8
(12' ceiling)

bath

BED RM.
11–0 x 12–0

pan.

(8' high wall)

cl

cl

master bath

pd. rm.

cl

w
d

lin.

BED RM.
12–0 x 11–0

walk-in closet

FOYER
6–0 x 7–4

cl

DINING
11–0 x 12–0
(12' ceiling)

© 1997 DONALD A. GARDNER
All rights reserved

STUDY/ BED RM.
11–4 x 12–0
(10' ceiling)

PORCH

GARAGE
21–8 x 22–10

Square Footage: 1,954

Width: 64'-10" Depth: 58'-10"

Graceful Archways

Enter this beautiful home through graceful archways and columns. The foyer, dining room and living room are one open space, defined by a creative room arrangement. The living room opens to the breakfast room and porch. The bedrooms are off a small hall reached through an archway. Two family bedrooms share a bath, while the master bedroom enjoys a private bath with a double-bowl vanity. A garage with storage and a utility room complete the floor plan. Please specify slab or crawlspace foundation when ordering.

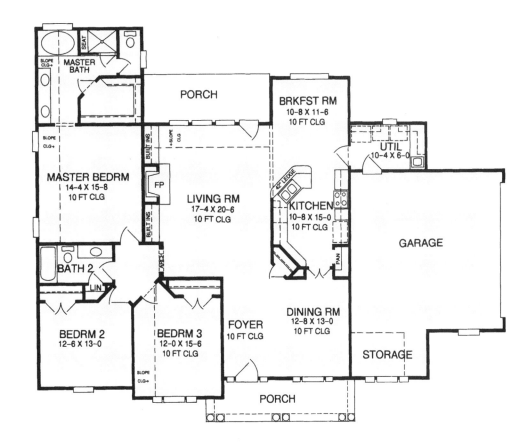

Square Footage: 1,932

Width: 53'-5" Depth: 65'-10"

Courtyard Patio with Spa

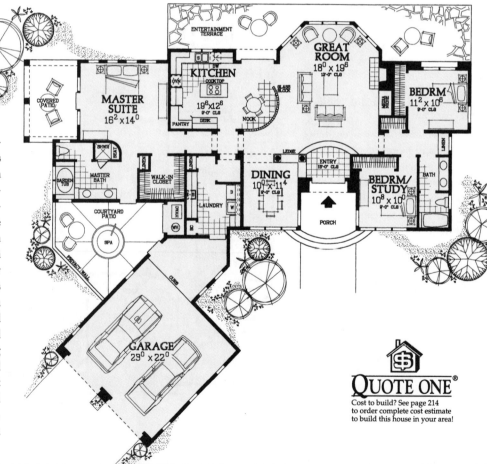

Here is a home designed to pamper family members and guests alike. The spacious great room combines with an entertainment terrace to make room for a crowd; formal meals will be a pleasure in the dining room. The U-shaped kitchen offers the cook plenty of extras, such as the built-in desk, corner pantry and cooktop island. Family members and friends will enjoy quiet meals in the eating nook, which is separated from the great room by a curved glass-block wall. Spend relaxing moments in the courtyard patio and spa. The master suite offers direct access to the courtyard patio as well as to its own private covered patio. Two family bedrooms (or a bedroom and a study) complete the plan.

Quote One®

Cost to build? See page 214 to order complete cost estimate to build this house in your area!

Square Footage: 2,085

Width: 82'-0" Depth: 75'-0"

DESIGN HPT880160

D ramatic interior angles provide for an immensely livable vacation plan that is metered with elegance enough for any social occasion. The open passage to the living room and formal dining room from the foyer is perfect for entertaining, while casual areas are positioned to the rear of the plan. The spacious kitchen, with extra storage at every turn, has an eat-in nook and a door to the rear patio. Three family bedrooms share a hall bath to complete this wing. The master suite is split from the family area to ensure a private retreat. The large bedroom can easily accommodate a sitting area and has a luxurious bath, walk-in closet and sliding doors to a private patio.

QUOTE ONE®
Cost to build? See page 214
to order complete cost estimate
to build this house in your area!

Square Footage: 2,612

Width: 93'-7" Depth: 74'-10"

L

Spa and Pool Area

Besides great curb appeal, this home has a wonderful floor plan. The foyer features a fountain that greets visitors and leads to a formal dining room on the right and a living room on the left. A large family room at the rear has a built-in entertainment center and a fireplace. The U-shaped kitchen is perfectly located for servicing all living and dining areas. To the right of the plan, away from the central entertaining spaces, are three family bedrooms sharing a full bath. On the left side, with solitude and comfort for the master suite, are a large sitting area, an office and an amenity-filled bath. A deck with a spa sits outside the master suite.

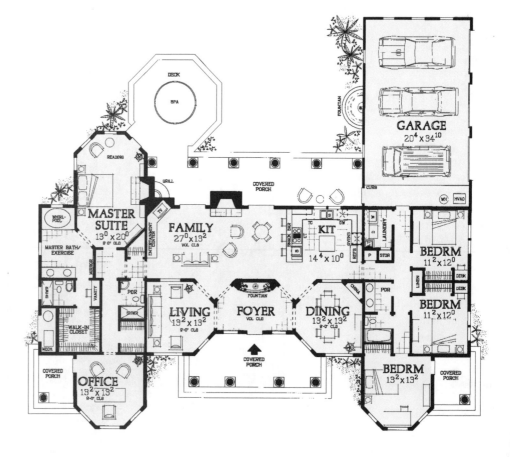

Square Footage: 2,831

Width: 84'-0" Depth: 77'-0"

DESIGN HPT880162

Guest Suite with Private Deck

Ensure an elegant lifestyle with this luxurious plan. A turret, two-story bay windows and plenty of arched glass impart a graceful style to the exterior, while rich amenities inside furnish contentment. A grand foyer decked with columns introduces the living room with curved-glass windows viewing the rear gardens. The study and living room share a through-fireplace. The master suite enjoys a tray ceiling, two walk-in closets, a separate shower and a garden tub set in a bay window. Informal entertainment will be a breeze with a rich leisure room adjoining the kitchen and breakfast nook and opening to a rear veranda. Upstairs, two family bedrooms and a guest suite with a private deck complete the plan.

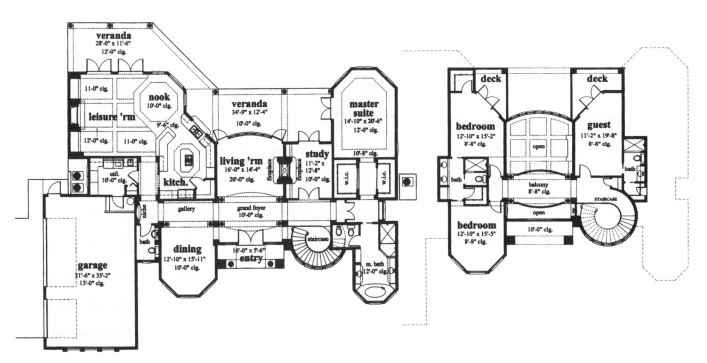

First Floor: 2,841 square feet
Second Floor: 1,052 square feet
Total: 3,893 square feet

Width: 85'-0" Depth: 76'-8"

Unbeatable Ambiance

This fresh and innovative design creates an unbeatable ambiance. The breakfast nook and family room both open to a patio—a perfect arrangement for informal entertaining. The dining room is sure to please with elegant pillars separating it from the sunken living room. A wet bar serves these formal rooms for entertainment events. A media room delights both with its shape and by being convenient to the nearby kitchen—great for snack runs. A private garden surrounds the master bath and its spa tub and enormous walk-in closet. The master bedroom is enchanting with a fireplace and access to the outdoors. Additional family bedrooms come in a variety of different shapes and sizes; Bedroom 4 reigns over the second floor and features its own full bath.

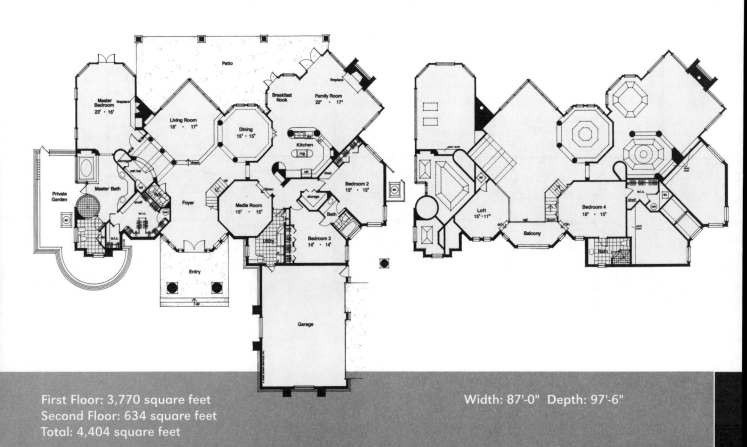

First Floor: 3,770 square feet
Second Floor: 634 square feet
Total: 4,404 square feet

Width: 87'-0" Depth: 97'-6"

J.V. HANSEN P.T.L.

DESIGN HPT880164

Curved Glass Wall

Patio

Master Bath

Master Bedroom
16⁸ · 13⁴

Pool

Spa

up

waterfall

down

Covered Patio

w.i.c.

wet bar

bar

down

Breakfast

Den Study
13⁴ · 11⁸

Bath

Living Room
19⁴ · 19⁰

Family Room
26⁸ · 14⁴

fireplace

Foyer

Entry

dw

up

Dining
13⁰ · 12⁰

Kitchen

pan

Utility

ref

w
d

Portico

ac wh

Double Garage

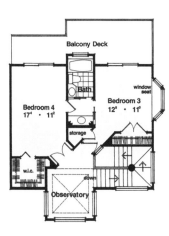

Balcony Deck

Bath

window seat

Bedroom 4
17⁴ · 11⁰

Bedroom 3
12⁸ · 11⁰

storage

w.i.c.

down

Observatory

As you drive up to the porte cochere entry of this home, the visual movement of the elevation is breathtaking. The multi-roofed spaces bring excitement the moment you walk through the double-doored entry. The foyer leads into the wide, glass-walled living room. To the right, the formal dining room features a tiered pedestal ceiling. To the left is the guest and master suite wing of the home. The master suite with its sweeping, curved glass wall has access to the patio area and overlooks the pool. The master bath, with its huge walk-in closet comes complete with a columned vanity area, a soaking tub and a shower for two.

First Floor: 2,212 square feet
Second Floor: 675 square feet
Total: 2,887 square feet

Width: 70'-0" Depth: 74'-1"

Ocean, Lake or Golf Course

Designed for a sloping lot, this fantastic Mediterranean home features all the views to the rear, making it the perfect home for an ocean, lake or golf-course view. Inside, the great room features a rear wall of windows. The breakfast room, kitchen, dining room and master suite also feature rear views. A three-level series of porches is located on the back for outdoor relaxing. Two bedroom suites are found upstairs, each with a private bath and a porch. The basement of this home features another bedroom suite and a large game room. An expandable area can be used as an office or Bedroom 5. This home may also be built with a slab foundation.

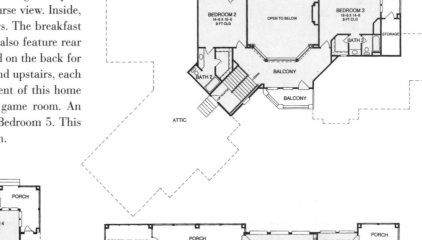

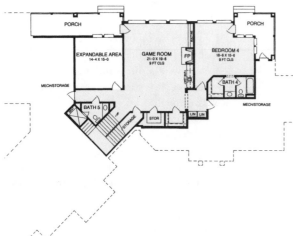

Main Level: 2,959 square feet
Upper Level: 1,055 square feet
Total: 4,014 square feet

Finished Basement: 1,270 square feet
Width: 110'-4" Depth: 72'-5"

DESIGN HPT880166

The striking facade of this magnificent estate is just the beginning of the excitement you will encounter inside. The entry foyer passes the formal dining room to the columned gallery, which leads to all regions of the house, with the formal living room at the focal point. The living room opens to the rear patio and the showpiece pool lying flush against the dramatic rear windows of the house. A sunken wet bar serves the living room and the pool via a swim-up bar. The outdoor kitchen is perfect for preparing summer meals. Back inside, the contemporary kitchen has a work island and all the amenities for gourmet preparation. The family room will be a favorite for casual entertainment.

Square Footage: 4,222
Bonus Space: 590 square feet

Width: 83'-10" Depth: 112'-0"

Octagonal Great Room

Villa enchantment is romantically enhanced by the facade of this Italianate design—Mediterranean allure creates the soft European appeal dressed in stucco attire. The wraparound entry porch is majestically inviting. Enter through double doors into the two-story foyer—notice the study with built-in cabinetry to the right and the formal dining room to the left. Straight ahead, an octagonal great room offers a fireplace, a built-in entertainment center and three sets of double doors, which lead outside to a vaulted lanai. The island kitchen is brightened by a bayed window and a pass-through to the lanai. Upstairs, a computer center and a morning kitchen are located at the end of the hallway, before opening onto the outer deck.

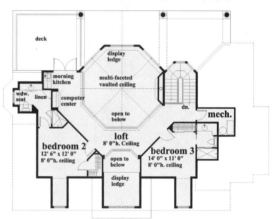

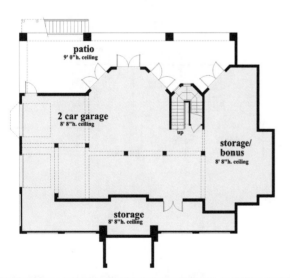

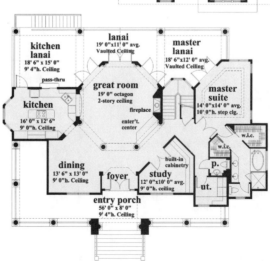

First Floor: 1,855 square feet
Second Floor: 901 square feet
Total: 2,756 square feet

Bonus Space: 1,010 square feet
Width: 66'-0" Depth: 50'-0"

DESIGN HPT880168

Island Living

This lovely pier home is the picture of island living. Space on the lower level is devoted to the garage, but allows for a storage area if needed. The first floor holds the great room, with access to a rear porch. The dining room and kitchen are nearby for easy access. The master suite is also on this floor and features porch access and a stunning bath. Two family bedrooms with private baths and a loft area are found on the second floor. A porch can be accessed from each of the bedrooms.

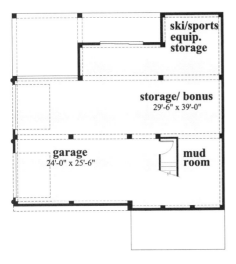

ski/sports equip. storage

storage/ bonus
29'-6" x 39'-0"

garage
24'-0" x 25'-6"

mud room

porch
30'-10" x 12'-8"
10' clg.

dining
12'-2" x 11'-4"
10' clg.

fireplace

great 'rm
16'-4" x 18'-0"
19'-4" clg.

kitch.
12'-2" x 13'-4"
10' clg.

master
13'-0" x 16'-0"
tray

niche

m. bath

w.i.c.

util.

porch
19'-8" x 8'-0"

open deck
30'-10" x 12'-8"

porch
8' clg.

porch
8' clg.

bedroom
12'-2" x 14'-0"
tray

bedroom
13'-2" x 12'-0"
tray

open

bath

w.i.c.

bath

loft
10'-4" x 11'-4"
8' clg.

open

First Floor: 1,492 square feet
Second Floor: 854 square feet
Total: 2,346 square feet

Bonus Space: 810 square feet
Width: 44'-0" Depth: 48'-0"

Beautiful Windows

Stone, stucco, beautiful windows and a tile roof all combine to give this home plenty of classy curb appeal. An elegant entry leads to the grand foyer, which introduces the formal living room. Here, a bowed wall of windows shows off the rear veranda, while a two-sided fireplace warms cool evenings. A cozy study shares the fireplace and offers access to the rear veranda. Providing privacy as well as pampering, the first-floor master suite is complete with two walk-in closets, a deluxe bath, a stepped ceiling and private access outdoors. For casual times, the leisure room features a fireplace, built-ins, a coffered ceiling and outdoor access. Upstairs, Bedrooms 2 and 3 share a bath, while the guest suite has a private bath. Please specify basement or slab foundation when ordering.

First Floor: 2,815 square feet
Second Floor: 1,091 square feet
Total: 3,906 square feet

Width: 85'-0" Depth: 76'-2"

DESIGN HPT880170

Stunning Veranda

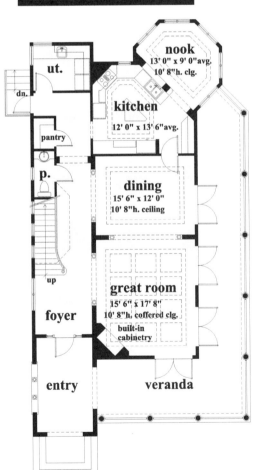

ut.

dn.

kitchen
12' 0" x 13' 6"avg.

nook
13' 0" x 9' 0"avg.
10' 8"h. clg.

pantry

p.

dining
15' 6" x 12' 0"
10' 8"h. ceiling

up

great room
15' 6" x 17' 8"
10' 8"h. coffered clg.

built-in cabinetry

foyer

entry

veranda

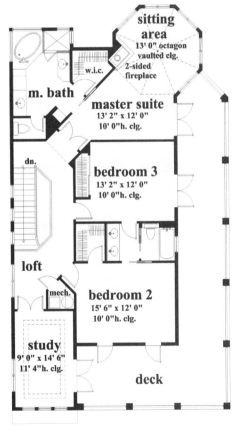

sitting area
13' 0" octagon
vaulted clg.

w.i.c.

2-sided fireplace

m. bath

master suite
13' 2" x 12' 0"
10' 0"h. clg.

dn.

bedroom 3
13' 2" x 12' 0"
10' 0"h. clg.

loft

mech.

bedroom 2
15' 6" x 12' 0"
10' 0"h. clg.

study
9' 0" x 14' 6"
11' 4"h. clg.

deck

This Casa Bellissima is pure Italianate elegance. Four double doors wrapping around the great room and dining area open to the stunning veranda. The great room is enhanced by a coffered ceiling and built-in cabinetry, while the entire first floor is bathed in sunlight from a wall of glass doors overlooking the veranda. The dining room connects to a gourmet island kitchen. Upstairs, a beautiful deck wraps gracefully around the family bedrooms. The master suite is a skylit haven enhanced by a bayed sitting area, which features a vaulted octagonal ceiling and a cozy two-sided fireplace. Private double doors access the sun deck from the master suite, Bedrooms 2 and 3 and the study.

First Floor: 1,266 square feet
Second Floor: 1,324 square feet
Total: 2,590 square feet

Width: 34'-0" Depth: 63'-2"

Spectacular Views

FIRST FLOOR / SECOND FLOOR

- DECK
- MASTER SUITE 13'-4" x 19'-6"
- LAKE LIVING 19'-10" x 15'-0"
- LAKE DINING 9'-6" x 13'-0"
- LAKE GATHERING 17'-0" x 18'-6"
- UP / DN
- KITCHEN 19'-6" x 16'-8"
- W.I.C.
- GALLERY
- P.
- MASTER BATH
- FOYER
- DINING ROOM 13'-4" x 12'-4"
- PDR.
- PORTICO
- L
- LAUNDRY

- BATH
- OPEN TO BELOW
- BATH
- SUITE 4 15'-0" x 16'-8"
- BALCONY
- DN
- ATTIC STOR.
- SUITE 3 13'-6" x 13'-0"
- OPEN TO BELOW
- SUITE 2 13'-4" x 13'-0"
- W.I.C.
- W.I.C.
- LEDGE
- ATTIC STOR.

- 2-CAR GARAGE 23'-0" x 20'-0"
- 1-CAR GARAGE 20'-0" x 12'-0"

- LOWER DECK
- LOUNGE 10'-0" x 10'-0"
- RECREATION ROOM 17'-6" x 26'-6"
- LOWER SUITE 13'-6" x 18'-6"
- GAME ROOM 20'-0" x 15'-0"
- UP
- BATH
- HALLWAY
- BOOK SHELVES
- BAR
- UNFIN. WORKSHOP 28'-0" x 13'-0"
- UNFIN. MECHANICAL 32'-6" x 9'-0"
- UNFIN. WINE CELLAR

This impressive Mediterranean design is dazzled in Italianate style. A front portico offers a warm welcome into the main level. The master suite is located to the left and includes rear-deck access, a double walk-in closet and pampering master bath. The island kitchen serves the formal and casual dining areas with ease. The casual gathering area is warmed by a fireplace. Three additional family suites reside upstairs, along with two baths and a balcony overlooking the two-story living room. The basement level adds a whole new layer of luxury, offering an additional suite, game room, recreation room, lounge area, wet bar and unfinished workshop and mechanical space for future use.

First Floor: 2,538 square feet
Second Floor: 1,171 square feet
Total: 3,709 square feet

Finished Basement: 1,784 square feet
Width: 67'-7" Depth: 85'-1"

DESIGN HPT880172

Show Stopper

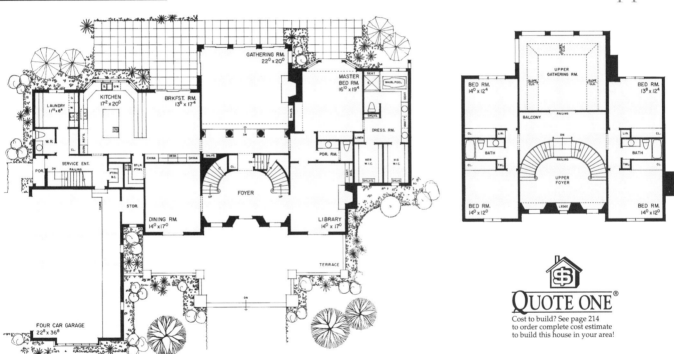

QUOTE ONE®
Cost to build? See page 214
to order complete cost estimate
to build this house in your area!

Reminiscent of a Mediterranean villa, this grand manor is a show stopper on the outside and a comfortable residence on the inside. An elegant receiving hall boasts a double staircase and is flanked by the formal dining room and the library. A huge gathering room at the back is graced by a fireplace and a wall of sliding glass doors to the rear terrace. The master bedroom resides on the first floor for privacy. With a lavish bath to pamper you and His and Hers walk-in closets, this suite will be a delight to retire to each evening. Upstairs are four additional bedrooms with ample storage space, a large balcony overlooking the gathering room and two full baths.

First Floor: 3,350 square feet
Second Floor: 1,298 square feet
Total: 4,648 square feet

Width: 97'-0" Depth: 74'-4"

French Country Manor

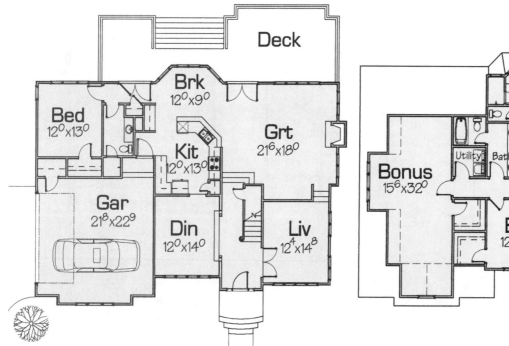

Deck

Brk
12⁰x9⁰

Bed
12⁰x13⁰

Grt
21⁶x18⁰

Kit
12⁰x13⁰

Gar
21⁸x22⁹

Din
12⁰x14⁰

Liv
12⁴x14⁸

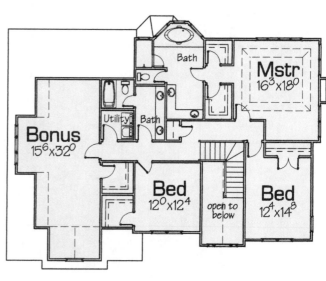

Bath

Mstr
16³x18⁰

Bonus
15⁶x32⁰

Utility

Bath

Bath

Bed
12⁰x12⁴

open to below

Bed
12⁴x14⁸

This elegant French country manor features a terraced main level that flows down to the great room, providing a sophisticated appeal that helps to further the dining, living and great room areas while also creating the ideal atmosphere for entertaining family and friends. Due to higher ceilings, the rear of the home features transom windows and a beautiful breakfast area that looks out onto the spacious rear deck. Adjacent is a private first-floor guest suite and full bath that could also serve as a study or home office. The second floor includes two additional bedrooms, a bonus room and a master suite, with tray ceilings, two walk-in closets and a luxurious bath with a large shower and a whirlpool tub.

First Floor: 1,602 square feet
Second Floor: 1,240 square feet
Total: 2,842 square feet

Bonus Space: 460 square feet
Width: 56'-8" Depth: 43'-0"

GRAND
European Manors

To view floor plans,
see page 21.

Two-Story Ceilings

Soaring ceiling heights allow full walls of glass for gorgeous views within this estate home. The grand salon, library and foyer all have two-story ceilings that expand on their already expansive areas. More intimate in ambience, the keeping room and attached morning room are designed for casual gatherings—and found near the kitchen for convenience. The kitchen features a curved work counter, a walk-in pantry and a built-in desk. Sharing a through-fireplace with the grand salon, the formal library is tucked away beyond gathering spaces. Sitting-room space complements the master suite where you will also find an exquisite bath and His and Hers walk-in closets. Twin staircases lead to four staterooms upstairs—each has a private bath.

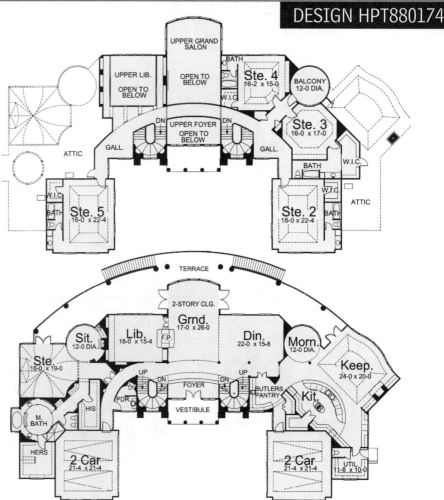

First Floor: 4,390 square feet
Second Floor: 2,452 square feet
Total: 6,842 square feet

Width: 131'-0" Depth: 73'-0"

DESIGN HPT880175

Spacious Master Suite

T his custom-designed estate home elegantly combines stone and stucco, arched windows and
stunning exterior details under its formidable hipped roof. The two-story foyer is impressive
with its grand staircase, tray ceiling and overlooking balcony. Equally remarkable is the generous living room with a fireplace and a coffered two-story ceiling. The kitchen, breakfast bay and
family room with a fireplace are all open to one another for a comfortable, casual atmosphere.
The first-floor master suite indulges with numerous closets, a dressing room and a fabulous bath.
Upstairs, four more bedrooms are topped by tray ceilings—three have walk-in closets and two
have private baths. The three-car garage boasts additional storage and a bonus room above.

First Floor: 3,520 square feet
Second Floor: 1,638 square feet
Total: 5,158 square feet

Bonus Room: 411 square feet
Width: 96'-6" Depth: 58'-8"

Lovely Flared Staircase

Elegantly styled in the French country tradition, this home features a well-thought-out floor plan with all the amenities. A large dining room and a study open off the two-story grand foyer that showcases a lovely flared staircase. A covered patio is accessed from the large formal living room. A more informal family room is conveniently located off the kitchen and breakfast room. The roomy master suite includes a sitting area, a luxurious private bath and its own entrance to the study. Three large bedrooms and a game room are located upstairs. Bedrooms 3 and 4 feature private dressing areas and a shared bath. Please specify basement or crawlspace foundation when ordering.

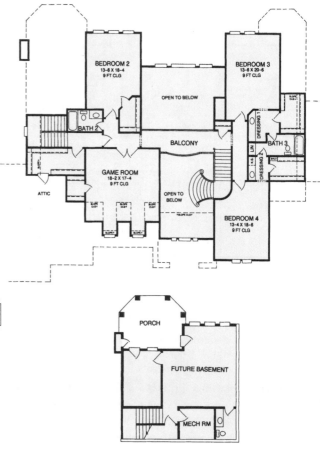

First Floor: 3,261 square feet
Second Floor: 1,920 square feet
Total: 5,181 square feet

Bonus Space: 710 square feet
Width: 86'-2" Depth: 66'-10"

DESIGN HPT880177

Sunken Grand Room

A stone-accented entrance welcomes you to this impressive French country estate. A sunken grand room combines with a bay-windowed dining room to create the formal living area. French doors open out to a multi-level terrace that links formal and informal areas and the master suite. A screened porch off the gathering room has a pass-through window from the kitchen to facilitate warm-weather dining. The master wing includes a study with a fireplace as well as a bayed sitting area and an amenity-laden bath. Two of the four bedrooms have private baths, while the others have separate dressing and vanity areas within a shared bath. A recreation room with a corner bar completes the plan.

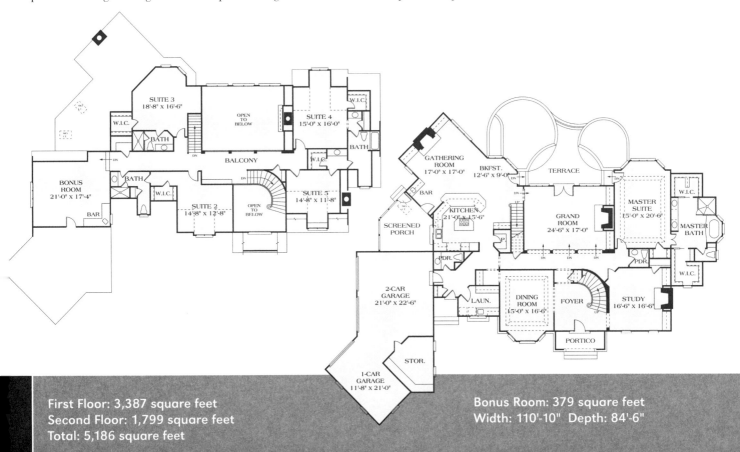

First Floor: 3,387 square feet
Second Floor: 1,799 square feet
Total: 5,186 square feet

Bonus Room: 379 square feet
Width: 110'-10" Depth: 84'-6"

Indoor Pool!

Stone and shutters on the outside are a prelude to the attractiveness of the interior of this French manor. Flanking the foyer is the formal dining room and two-story study—complete with a fireplace and spiral staircase to the study loft. The grand room is aptly named, with a second fireplace and direct access to the rear covered terrace. A third fireplace is shared with the family room and a covered porch. A lavish master suite is designed to pamper with a huge walk-in closet and a luxurious bath offering direct access to the indoor pool! Upstairs, four suites—each with a walk-in closet—share three bathrooms and access to the study loft.

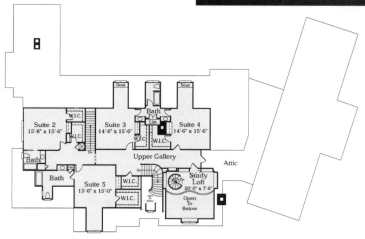

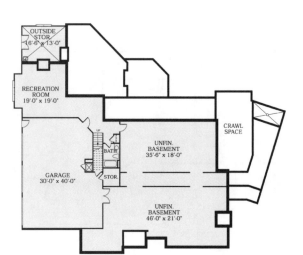

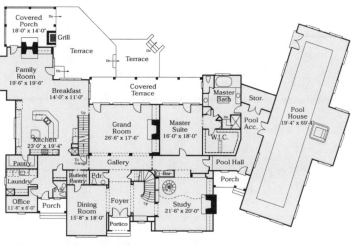

First Floor: 4,002 square feet
Second Floor: 2,338 square feet
Total: 6,340 square feet

Finished Basement: 652 square feet
Pool House: 2,079 square feet
Width: 133'-4" Depth: 84'-0"

DESIGN HPT880179

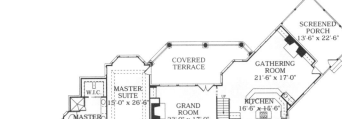

SCREENED PORCH 13'-6" x 22'-6"

COVERED TERRACE

GATHERING ROOM 21'-6" x 17'-0"

MASTER SUITE 15'-0" x 26'-6"

W.I.C.

MASTER BATH

GRAND ROOM 23'-0" x 17'-0"

KITCHEN 16'-6" x 15'-6"

UP

W.I.C.

PDR.

GALLERY

PDR.

BUTLER'S PANTRY

2 CAR GARAGE 24'-0" x 22'-6"

STUDY 15'-6" x 15'-6"

DINING ROOM 14'-0" x 14'-6"

LAUN.

UP

FOYER

PORTICO

MECH./ STOR. 16'-6" x 16'-0"

1 CAR GARAGE 11'-6" x 23'-0"

SUITE 5 15'-0" x 16'-0"

SUITE 3 18'-10" x 17'-4"

W.I.C.

BATH

OPEN TO BELOW

W.I.C.

BATH

BATH

W.I.C.

BALCONY

DN

BATH

SUITE 4 13'-8" x 11'-0"

DN

W.I.C.

BOOK SHELVES

SUITE 2 14'-0" x 15'-4"

OPEN TO BELOW

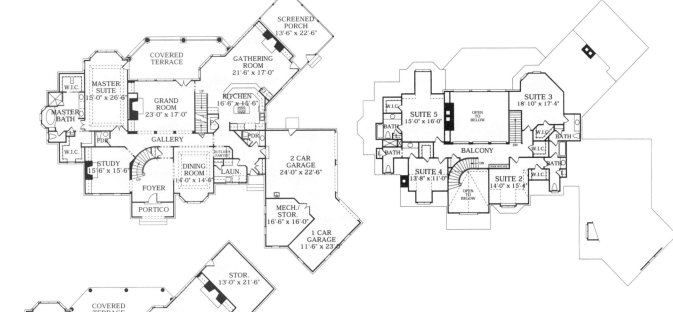

STOR. 13'-0" x 21'-6"

COVERED TERRACE

GAME ROOM 21'-6" x 17'-0"

BATH

SUITE 6 15'-0" x 20'-0"

RECREATION ROOM 23'-0" x 17'-0"

UP

PDR.

WET BAR

COMPUTER ROOM 12'-6" x 13'-0"

W.I.C.

W.I.C.

W.I.C.

MECH./ STOR.

FUTURE HOME THEATER

Three levels of luxury highlight the livability of this French Country manor. A formal portico welcomes you inside to a foyer that introduces a beautiful curved staircase. To the left, the study features a fireplace with flanking built-ins. To the right, the formal dining room is easily served from the island kitchen. The grand room presents a massive hearth and accesses the rear terrace. The gathering room and nook are also warmed by a fireplace and access a rear screened porch. The first-floor master suite provides a private bath and two walk-in closets. Upstairs, a balcony overlooks the grand room below. Four additional family bedrooms reside on this level.

First Floor: 3,309 square feet
Second Floor: 1,694 square feet
Total: 5,003 square feet

Finished Basement: 2,235 square feet
Width: 112'-9" Depth: 97'-0"

Massive Fireplace

Both formal and informal spaces grace the floor plan of this Tudor one-story home. A grand entry opens to the formal dining room and, nearby, French doors lead to a quiet library or study. The heart of the home is a spacious living room with a tray ceiling and a massive fireplace. The master suite and one family bedroom sit on the left side of the plan, while two additional bedrooms reside on the right. The family room has a beam ceiling and cozy fireplace. Bonus space over the garage adds 774 square feet.

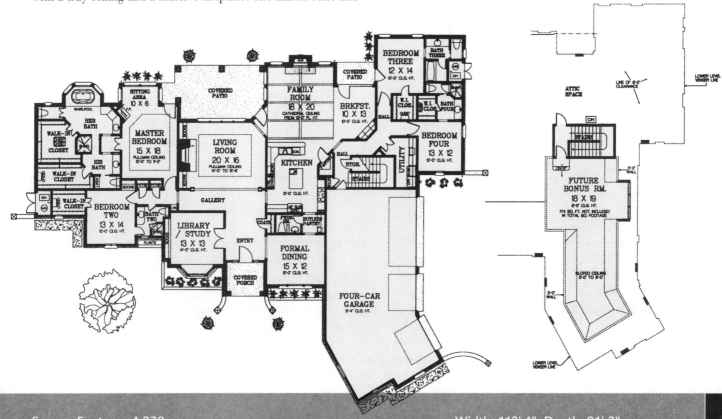

Square Footage: 4,270
Bonus Space: 774 square feet

Width: 112'-4" Depth: 91'-3"

DESIGN HPT880181

Home Theater and Office

Gables, varied rooflines, interesting dormers, arched windows, a recessed entry—the detailing on this stone manor is exquisite! The foyer opens through arches to the formal dining room, an elegant stair hall and the grand room, with its fireplace, built-ins and French doors to the lanai. The informal zone includes a kitchen with an oversized work island and pantry, a breakfast nook and a family room with a fireplace and its own screened porch. An anteroom outside the master suite gives the homeowners added privacy and allows the option of a private entrance to the study. The master bath is loaded with extras, including a stairway to the upstairs exercise room. The second floor also offers a home theater and a home office, as well as four bedroom suites and a mother-in-law or maid's apartment. Note that there are four sets of stairs to aid in the traffic flow and a laundry room on each level.

First Floor: 5,200 square feet
Second Floor: 4,177 square feet
Total: 9,377 square feet

Width: 155'-9" Depth: 107'-11"

A Gourmet's Delight

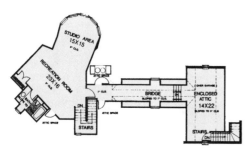

From the master bedroom suite to the detached four-car garage, this design will delight even the most discerning palates. While the formal living and dining rooms bid greeting as you enter, the impressive great room, with its cathedral ceiling, raised-hearth fireplace and veranda access, will take your breath away. A gallery hall leads to the kitchen and the family sleeping wing on the right and to the study, guest suite and master suite on the left. The large island kitchen, with its sunny breakfast nook, will be a gourmet's delight. The master suite includes a bayed sitting area, a dual fireplace shared with the study, and a luxurious bath. Each additional bedroom features its own bath and sitting area.

First Floor: 5,152 square feet
Second Floor: 726 square feet
Total: 5,878 square feet

Width: 146'-7" Depth: 106'-7"

DESIGN HPT880184

Shake-covered dormers, segmented lintels and stone accents highlight this brick country home. Tall chimneys support three fireplaces—in the gathering room, the grand room and the study. Distinctive features include built-ins flanking the fireplaces, a large work island and walk-in pantry in the kitchen, and a laundry room with plenty of counter space for sorting and folding. The master suite offers private access to the terrace, two huge walk-in closets and His and Hers baths sharing only the tub and shower area. Three flights of stairs lead upstairs to four family bedroom suites with private baths, a home theater and bonus space over one of the two-car garages.

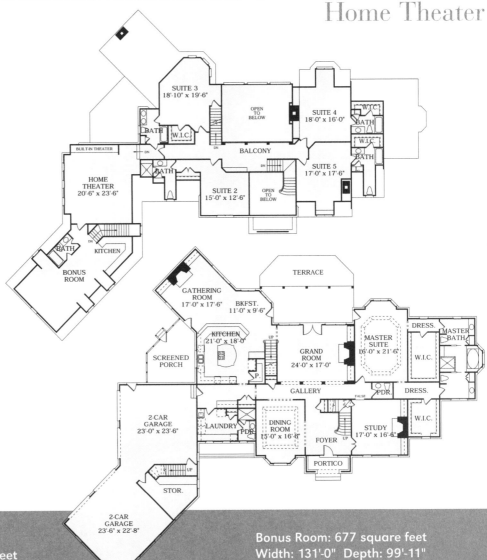

First Floor: 3,767 square feet
Second Floor: 2,602 square feet
Total: 6,369 square feet

Bonus Room: 677 square feet
Width: 131'-0" Depth: 99'-11"

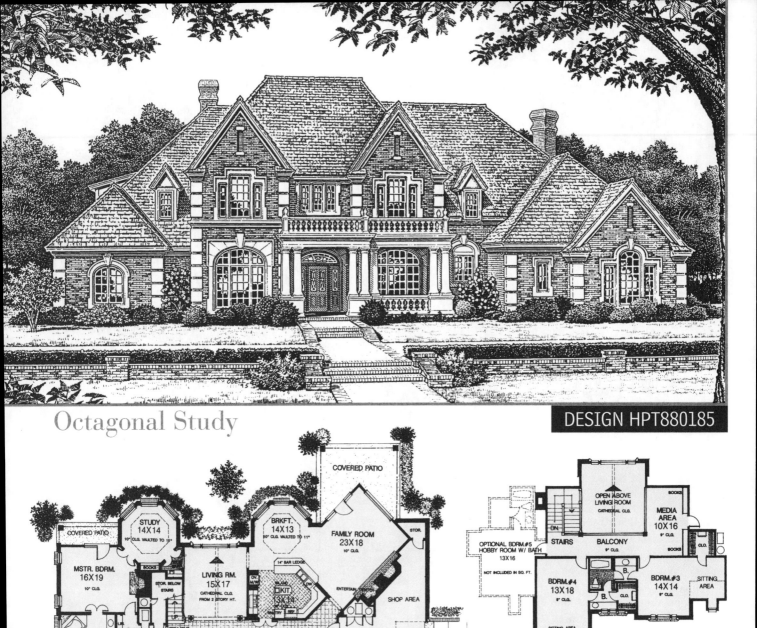

Octagonal Study

© Copyright Fillmore Design Group.

S tucco corner quoins, multiple gables and graceful columns all combine to give this European manor plenty of appeal. Inside, a gallery entry presents a formal dining room on the right, defined by elegant columns, while the formal living room awaits just ahead. The highly efficient kitchen features a worktop island, pantry and a serving bar to the nearby octagonal breakfast area. The family room offers a built-in entertainment center, a fireplace and its own covered patio. The left side of the first floor is dedicated to the master suite. Here, the homeowner is pampered with an octagonal study, huge walk-in closet, lavish bath and a very convenient nursery. The second floor contains two family bedrooms, each with a walk-in closet, and a media area with built-in bookshelves.

First Floor: 3,168 square feet
Second Floor: 998 square feet
Total: 4,166 square feet

Width: 90'-0" Depth: 63'-5"

DESIGN HPT880186

Striking Touches

Brick detailing, multiple gables, a grand entrance and many other striking touches all combine to produce an elegant home you will love to live in. Inside, the foyer is flanked by the formal living room to the right—complete with a fireplace—and a formal dining room on the left. The spacious great room offers a second fireplace as well as built-ins and a wall of windows. The kitchen will surely please the gourmet of the family,

with its work island, walk-in pantry and double oven. A guest bedroom is also on this floor, providing plenty of privacy for guests. The lavish master suite is full of amenities, including a walk-in closet with built-ins and ten-foot ceilings, a deluxe bath with a whirlpool tub, and a fireplace, bayed sitting area and private outdoor access in the bedroom.

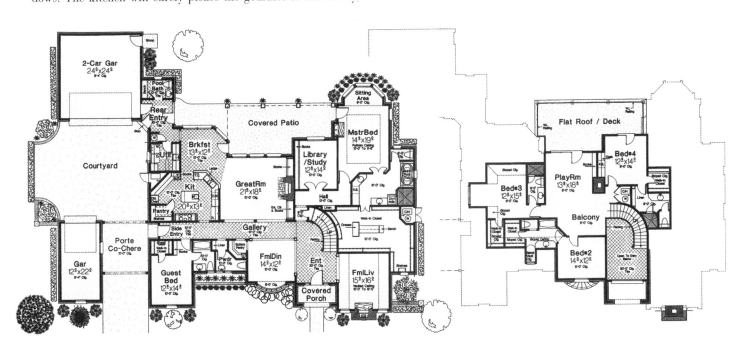

First Floor: 3,538 square feet
Second Floor: 1,432 square feet
Total: 4,970 square feet

Width: 102'-10" Depth: 77'-10"

Stately Tudor Home

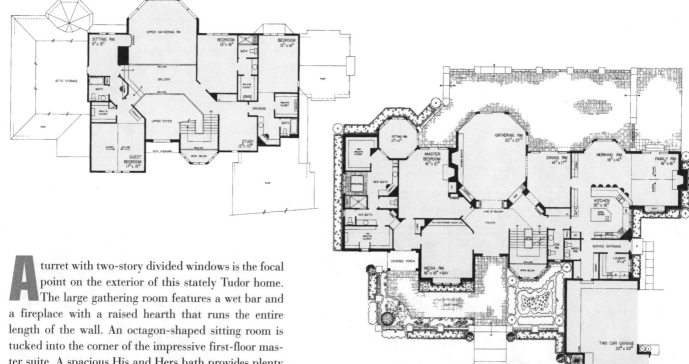

A turret with two-story divided windows is the focal point on the exterior of this stately Tudor home. The large gathering room features a wet bar and a fireplace with a raised hearth that runs the entire length of the wall. An octagon-shaped sitting room is tucked into the corner of the impressive first-floor master suite. A spacious His and Hers bath provides plenty of room with two walk-in closets, compartmented commodes and vanities and a separate tub. Three bedrooms—one a guest suite with a sitting room—three baths and a study are located on the second floor.

First Floor: 4,195 square feet
Second Floor: 2,094 square feet
Total: 6,289 square feet

Width: 111'-4" Depth: 87'-6"

DESIGN HPT880188

Enchanted Chateau

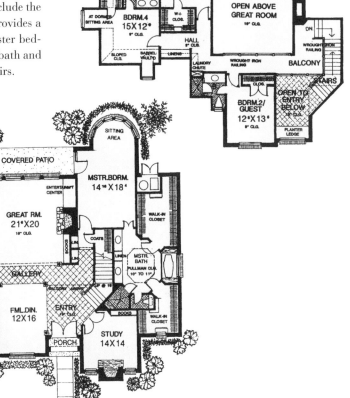

This enchanted Chateau sings of refined European luxury. A formal dining room and study flank the entry. A massive stone fireplace warms the great room, which provides a wall of glass with views to the covered patio and beyond to the rear property. Casual areas include the kitchen, breakfast and recreation rooms. A deluxe tiled kitchen provides a snack counter that overlooks a beautiful morning nook. The master bedroom is a sumptuous retreat with a bayed sitting area, pampering bath and two walk-in closets. Three additional bedrooms are located upstairs.

First Floor: 2,995 square feet
Second Floor: 1,102 square feet
Total: 4,097 square feet

Width: 120'-6" Depth: 58'-8"

© Sater Design Collection, Inc.

Octagonal Breakfast Nook

Elegance is well displayed on this European manor by its stone and stucco facade, multiple-pane windows, grand entrance and varied rooflines. The grand foyer introduces the formal dining room on the left and a spacious formal living room directly ahead. The study and living room share a through-fireplace, and both have access to the backyard. The kitchen features a walk-in pantry, a cooktop island, a pass-through to the rear veranda and an adjacent octagonal breakfast nook. Nearby, the leisure room is complete with a coffered ceiling, built-ins and another fireplace. The master suite resides on the right side of the home, and provides two walk-in closets and a lavish bath. Please specify basement or slab foundation when ordering.

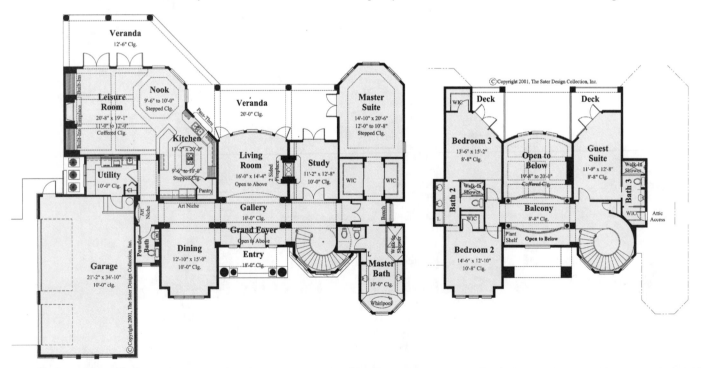

First Floor: 2,794 square feet
Second Floor: 1,127 square feet
Total: 3,921 square feet

Width: 85'-0" Depth: 76'-2"

DESIGN HPT880190

Magnificent Master Suite

A steeply pitched roof, a generous supply of multi-pane windows, and fanlights and glass side panels that accent the front entry enhance the grand design of this beautiful home. Highlights include a magnificent first-floor master suite, a sun-filled living room overlooking the rear grounds and bay windows in the family room, dining room and study. The kitchen features a central food-preparation island, wrapping counters and a pantry. The adjoining breakfast area provides access to the rear veranda, which also leads to the family room. Upstairs, two secondary bedrooms share a full bath, while a guest suite offers lavish amenities.

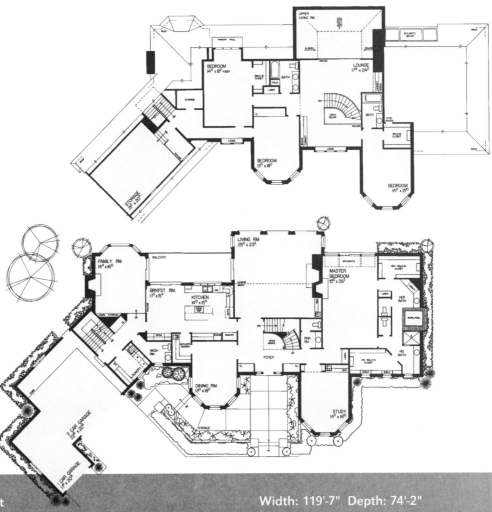

First Floor: 3,644 square feet
Second Floor: 2,005 square feet
Total: 5,649 square feet

Width: 119'-7"   Depth: 74'-2"

Spectacular Panorama

The design of this Country French estate captures its ambiance with its verandas, grand entry and unique balconies. A spectacular panorama of the formal living areas and the elegant curved stairway awaits just off the foyer. A large island kitchen, breakfast nook and family room will impress, as will the breakfast nook and wine cellar. Plenty of kitchen pantry space leads to the laundry and motor court featuring a two-car garage attached to the main house and a three-car garage attached by a breezeway. The master suite boasts a sunken sitting area with a see-through fireplace, His and Hers walk-in closets, island tub and large separate shower. A study area, three additional bedrooms, full bath and a bonus area reside on the second floor.

First Floor: 3,517 square feet
Second Floor: 1,254 square feet
Total: 4,771 square feet

Width: 95'-8" Depth: 107'-0"

DESIGN HPT880192

Three Fireplaces

Stone accents and an eccentric curved roofline lend this stucco design the look of a cottage, but the interior is definitely that of a manor house. An elegant curved stairway accents the foyer, which opens to a study to the left and a formal dining room to the right. The beam-ceilinged living room is perfect for entertaining, with one of three fireplaces in the house and access to a covered terrace. The family room features a glass-walled turret, which is echoed as a sitting room in the master suite. The master retreat also boasts a morning kitchen, two walk-in closets and a wonderful bath. Completing the plan are four more bedrooms and an apartment over the garage for a nanny or a college student.

SUITE 5
15'-0" x 15'-0"

SUITE 4
11'-8" x 17'-4"

BATH

SUITE 3
12'-0" x 17'-0"

W.I.C. W.I.C.

UPPER GALLERY

W.I.C. BATH

BALCONY

OPEN TO BELOW

SUITE 2
15'-0" x 14'-6"

BATH

BALCONY

BALCONY

OPEN TO BELOW

RECREATION ROOM
23'-6" x 16'-0"

KITCHEN
7'-8" x 11'-6"

BATH

APT.
15'-0" x 30'-6"

SITTING ROOM

MORNING KITCHEN

COVERED TERRACE

MASTER SUITE
20'-0" x 18'-0"

MASTER BATH

ANTE RM.

PDR

W.I.C. W.I.C.

GALLERY

FOYER

STUDY
17'-0" x 14'-8"

PORTICO

LIVING ROOM
22'-6" x 17'-6"

FAMILY ROOM
27'-8" x 23'-8"

KITCHEN
23'-8" x 20'-0"

PANT.

PDR

DINING ROOM
15'-0" x 15'-0"

LAUN.

PORCH

UP

DN

UP

UP

3-CAR GARAGE
26'-0" x 34'-4"

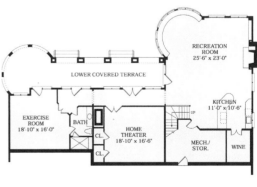

LOWER COVERED TERRACE

EXERCISE ROOM
18'-10" x 16'-0"

BATH

CL.

CL.

HOME THEATER
18'-10" x 16'-6"

MECH./ STOR.

WINE

RECREATION ROOM
25'-6" x 23'-0"

KITCHEN
11'-0" x 10'-6"

First Floor: 4,143 square feet
Second Floor: 2,392 square feet
Total: 6,535 square feet

Apartment: 638 square feet
Width: 117'-6" Depth: 98'-2"

Studio Apartment

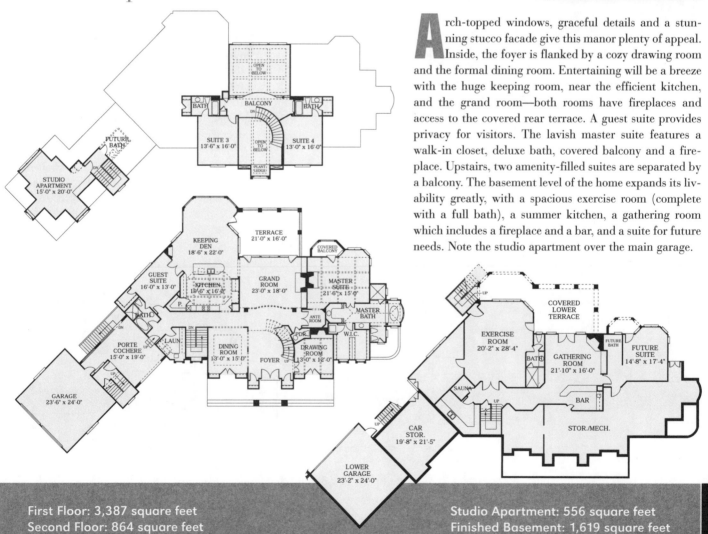

rch-topped windows, graceful details and a stunning stucco facade give this manor plenty of appeal. Inside, the foyer is flanked by a cozy drawing room and the formal dining room. Entertaining will be a breeze with the huge keeping room, near the efficient kitchen, and the grand room—both rooms have fireplaces and access to the covered rear terrace. A guest suite provides privacy for visitors. The lavish master suite features a walk-in closet, deluxe bath, covered balcony and a fireplace. Upstairs, two amenity-filled suites are separated by a balcony. The basement level of the home expands its livability greatly, with a spacious exercise room (complete with a full bath), a summer kitchen, a gathering room which includes a fireplace and a bar, and a suite for future needs. Note the studio apartment over the main garage.

First Floor: 3,387 square feet
Second Floor: 864 square feet
Total: 4,251 square feet

Studio Apartment: 556 square feet
Finished Basement: 1,619 square feet
Width: 127'-9" Depth: 75'-8"

DESIGN HPT880194

Spacious Sun Room

A distinctively French flair is the hallmark of this European design. Inside, the two-story foyer offers views to the huge great room beyond. A well-placed study off the foyer provides space for a home office. The kitchen, breakfast room and sun room are adjacent to lend a spacious feel. The great room is visible from this area through decorative arches. The master suite includes a roomy sitting area and a lovely bath with a centerpiece whirlpool tub flanked by half-columns. Upstairs, Bedrooms 2 and 3 share a bath that includes separate dressing areas. Please specify crawlspace or slab foundation when ordering.

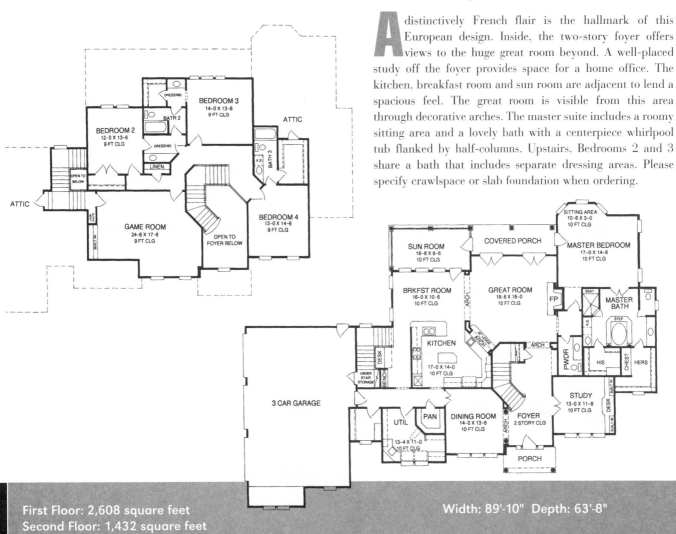

First Floor: 2,608 square feet
Second Floor: 1,432 square feet
Total: 4,040 square feet

Width: 89'-10" Depth: 63'-8"

Music Alcove

Graceful window arches soften the massive chimneys and hipped roof of this grand European manor dazzled in French highlights. Inside, a two-story gathering room is just two steps down from the adjacent lounge with an impressive wet bar and a semi-circular music alcove. This area is reserved for elegant entertaining or decadent relaxation. The highly effi-

cient galley-style kitchen overlooks the family-room fireplace and spectacular windowed breakfast room. The rear terrace is perfect for outdoor entertaining. The master suite is a private retreat with a fireplace and a wood box tucked into the corner of its sitting room. Separate His-and-Hers baths and dressing rooms guarantee plenty of space and privacy.

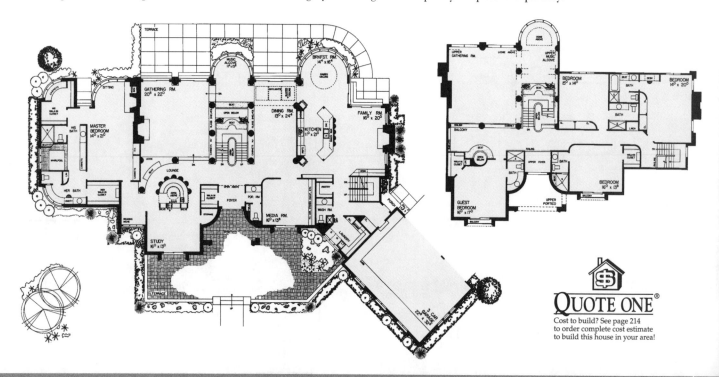

Quote One®

Cost to build? See page 214
to order complete cost estimate
to build this house in your area!

First Floor: 4,786 square feet
Second Floor: 1,842 square feet
Total: 6,628 square feet

Width: 133'-8" Depth: 87'-10"
L **D**

DESIGN HPT880196

The exterior of this magnificent baronial Tudor conceals an interior fit for royalty. The two-story foyer reveals a circular staircase housed in a turret plus a powder room and a telephone center located for easy use by guests. Two steps lead down to the elegant living room with its music alcove or to the sumptuous library with a wet bar. Both rooms offer fireplaces, as does the family room. The kitchen is a chef's delight, with a large work island, a snack bar and a butler's pantry leading into the formal dining room. The second floor features four family bedrooms, two with fireplaces, and each with a private bath. Adjacent to the master suite is a nursery that would also make an ideal exercise room.

Quote One®

Cost to build? See page 214 to order complete cost estimate to build this house in your area!

First Floor: 3,840 square feet
Second Floor: 3,435 square feet
Total: 7,275 square feet

Width: 133'-9" Depth: 85'-6"

Two Guest Suites

DESIGN HPT880197

This country estate leaves nothing out when it comes to luxurious living. The uniquely beautiful front portico leads to a sunlit foyer with an elegant curved stair. Special features on the first floor include a bar in the dining room, a private guest room near the spacious kitchen, a covered lanai leading to multiple terraces, a private study with a fireplace and a master suite with separate His and Hers bathrooms. Besides housing two guest suites, the second floor is available for fun and leisure with a study loft, a private studio with a built-in darkroom, a home theater with a bar and a large recreation room.

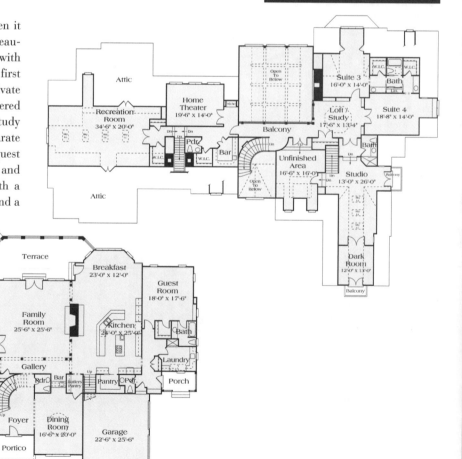

First Floor: 6,158 square feet
Second Floor: 4,090 square feet
Total: 10,248 square feet

Bonus Space: 715 square feet
Width: 136'-4" Depth: 99'-10"

LET US SHOW YOU
OUR HOME BLUEPRINT PACKAGE.

BUILDING A HOME? PLANNING A HOME?
OUR BLUEPRINT PACKAGE HAS NEARLY EVERYTHING YOU NEED TO GET THE JOB DONE RIGHT,

whether you're working on your own or with help from an architect, designer, builder or subcontractors. Each Blueprint Package is the result of many hours of work by licensed architects or professional designers.

QUALITY

Hundreds of hours of painstaking effort have gone into the development of your blueprint plan. Each home has been quality checked by professionals to insure accuracy and buildability.

VALUE

Because we sell in volume, you can buy professional quality blueprints at a fraction of their development cost. With our plans, your dream home design costs substantially less than the fees charged by architects.

SERVICE

Once you've chosen your favorite home plan, you'll receive fast, efficient service whether you choose to mail or fax your order to us or call us toll free at 1-800-521-6797. After you have received your order, call for customer service toll free 1-888-690-1116.

SATISFACTION

Over 50 years of service to satisfied home plan buyers provide us unparalleled experience and knowledge in producing quality blueprints.

ORDER TOLL FREE 1-800-521-6797

After you've looked over our Blueprint Package and Important Extras, call toll free on our Blueprint Hotline: 1-800-521-6797, for current pricing and availability prior to mailing the order form on page 221. We're ready and eager to serve you. After you have received your order, call for customer service toll free 1-888-690-1116.

Each set of blueprints is an interrelated collection of detail sheets which includes components such as floor plans, interior and exterior elevations, dimensions, cross-sections, diagrams and notations. These sheets show exactly how your house is to be built.

SETS MAY INCLUDE:

FRONTAL SHEET
This artist's sketch of the exterior of the house gives you an idea of how the house will look when built and landscaped. Large floor plans show all levels of the house and provide an overview of your new home's livability, as well as a handy reference for deciding on furniture placement.

FOUNDATION PLANS
This sheet shows the foundation layout including support walls, excavated and unexcavated areas, if any, and foundation notes. If slab construction rather than basement, the plan shows footings and details for a monolithic slab. This page, or another in the set, may include a sample plot plan for locating your house on a building site.

DETAILED FLOOR PLANS
These plans show the layout of each floor of the house. Rooms and interior spaces are carefully dimensioned and keys are given for cross-section details provided later in the plans. The positions of electrical outlets and switches are shown.

HOUSE CROSS-SECTIONS
Large-scale views show sections or cut-aways of the foundation, interior walls, exterior walls, floors, stairways and roof details. Additional cross-sections may show important changes in floor, ceiling or roof heights or the relationship of one level to another. Extremely valuable for construction, these sections show exactly how the various parts of the house fit together.

INTERIOR ELEVATIONS
Many of our drawings show the design and placement of kitchen and bathroom cabinets, laundry areas, fireplaces, bookcases and other built-ins. Little "extras," such as mantelpiece and wainscoting drawings, plus molding sections, provide details that give your home that custom touch.

EXTERIOR ELEVATIONS
These drawings show the front, rear and sides of your house and give necessary notes on exterior materials and finishes. Particular attention is given to cornice detail, brick and stone accents or other finish items that make your home unique.

IMPORTANT EXTRAS TO DO THE JOB RIGHT!

INTRODUCING IMPORTANT PLANNING AND CONSTRUCTION AIDS DEVELOPED BY OUR PROFESSIONALS TO HELP YOU SUCCEED IN YOUR HOME-BUILDING PROJECT

MATERIALS LIST

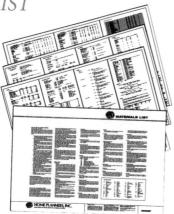

(Note: Because of the diversity of local building codes, our Materials List does not include mechanical materials.)

For many of the designs in our portfolio, we offer a customized materials take-off that is invaluable in planning and estimating the cost of your new home. This Materials List outlines the quantity, type and size of materials needed to build your house (with the exception of mechanical system items). Included are framing lumber, windows and doors, kitchen and bath cabinetry, rough and finish hardware, and much more. This handy list helps you or your builder cost out materials and serves as a reference sheet when you're compiling bids. Some Materials Lists may be ordered before blueprints are ordered, call for information.

SPECIFICATION OUTLINE

This valuable 16-page document is critical to building your house correctly. Designed to be filled in by you or your builder, this book lists 166 stages or items crucial to the building process. It provides a comprehensive review of the construction process and helps in choosing materials. When combined with the blueprints, a signed contract, and a schedule, it becomes a legal document and record for the building of your home.

QUOTE ONE®

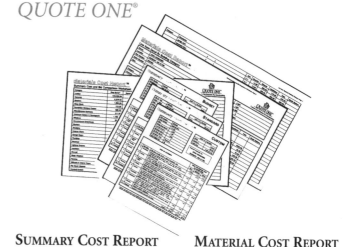

SUMMARY COST REPORT   **MATERIAL COST REPORT**

A product for estimating the cost of building select designs, the Quote One® system is available in two separate stages: The Summary Cost Report and the Material Cost Report.

The **Summary Cost Report** is the first stage in the package and shows the total cost per square foot for your chosen home in your zip-code area and then breaks that cost down into various categories showing the costs for building materials, labor and installation. The report includes three grades: Budget, Standard and Custom. These reports allow you to evaluate your building budget and compare the costs of building a variety of homes in your area.

Make even more informed decisions about your home-building project with the second phase of our package, our **Material Cost Report.** This tool is invaluable in planning and estimating the cost of your new home. The material and installation (labor and equipment) cost is shown for each of over 1,000 line items provided in the Materials List (Standard grade), which is included when you purchase this estimating tool. It allows you to determine building costs for your specific zip-code area and for your chosen home design. Space is allowed for additional estimates from contractors and subcontractors, such as for mechanical materials, which are not included in our packages. This invaluable tool includes a Materials List. A Material Cost Report cannot be ordered before blueprints are ordered. Call for details. In addition, ask about our Home Planners Estimating Package.

If you are interested in a plan that is not indicated as Quote One®, please call and ask our sales reps. They will be happy to verify the status for you. To order these invaluable reports, use the order form.

214

CONSTRUCTION INFORMATION

IF YOU WANT TO KNOW MORE ABOUT TECHNIQUES— and deal more confidently with subcontractors — we offer these useful sheets. Each set is an excellent tool that will add to your understanding of these technical subjects. These helpful details provide general construction information and are not specific to any single plan.

PLUMBING

The Blueprint Package includes locations for all the plumbing fixtures, including sinks, lavatories, tubs, showers, toilets, laundry trays and water heaters. However, if you want to know more about the complete plumbing system, these Plumbing Details will prove very useful. Prepared to meet requirements of the National Plumbing Code, these fact-filled sheets give general information on pipe schedules, fittings, sump-pump details, water-softener hookups, septic system details and much more. Sheets also include a glossary of terms.

ELECTRICAL

The locations for every electrical switch, plug and outlet are shown in your Blueprint Package. However, these Electrical Details go further to take the mystery out of household electrical systems. Prepared to meet requirements of the National Electrical Code, these comprehensive drawings come packed with helpful information, including wire sizing, switch-installation schematics, cable-routing details, appliance wattage, doorbell hook-ups, typical service panel circuitry and much more. A glossary of terms is also included.

CONSTRUCTION

The Blueprint Package contains information an experienced builder needs to construct a particular house. However, it doesn't show all the ways that houses can be built, nor does it explain alternate construction methods. To help you understand how your house will be built—and offer additional techniques—this set of Construction Details depicts the materials and methods used to build foundations, fireplaces, walls, floors and roofs. Where appropriate, the drawings show acceptable alternatives.

MECHANICAL

These Mechanical Details contain fundamental principles and useful data that will help you make informed decisions and communicate with subcontractors about heating and cooling systems. Drawings contain instructions and samples that allow you to make simple load calculations, and preliminary sizing and costing analysis. Covered are the most commonly used systems from heat pumps to solar fuel systems. The package is filled with illustrations and diagrams to help you visualize components and how they relate to one another.

THE HANDS-ON HOME FURNITURE PLANNER

Effectively plan the space in your home using The **Hands-On Home Furniture Planner**. It's fun and easy—no more moving heavy pieces of furniture to see how the room will go together. And you can try different layouts, moving furniture at a whim.

The kit includes reusable peel and stick furniture templates that fit onto a 12" x 18" laminated layout board—space enough to layout every room in your home.

Also included in the package are a number of helpful planning tools. You'll receive:

✓ Helpful hints and solutions for difficult situations.
✓ Furniture planning basics to get you started.
✓ Furniture planning secrets that let you in on some of the tricks of professional designers.

The **Hands-On Home Furniture Planner** is the one tool that no new homeowner or home remodeler should be without. It's also a perfect housewarming gift!

To Order, Call Toll Free
1-800-521-6797

After you've looked over our Blueprint Package and Important Extras on these pages, call for current pricing and availability prior to mailing the order form. We're ready and eager to serve you. After you have received your order, call for customer service toll free 1-888-690-1116.

The Finishing Touches...

THE DECK BLUEPRINT PACKAGE

Many of the homes in this book can be enhanced with a professionally designed Home Planners Deck Plan. Those homes marked with a **D** have a complementary Deck Plan, sold separately, which includes a Deck Plan Frontal Sheet, Deck Framing and Floor Plans, Deck Elevations and a Deck Materials List. A Standard Deck Details Package, also available, provides all the how-to information necessary for building *any* deck. Our Complete Deck Building Package contains one set of Custom Deck Plans of your choice, plus one set of Standard Deck Building Details, all for one low price. Our plans and details are carefully prepared in an easy-to-understand format that will guide you through every stage of your deck-building project. This page shows a sample Deck layout to match your favorite house. See Blueprint Price Schedule for ordering information.

THE LANDSCAPE BLUEPRINT PACKAGE

For the homes marked with an **L** in this book, Home Planners has created a front-yard Landscape Plan that is complementary in design to the house plan. These comprehensive blueprint packages include a Frontal Sheet, Plan View, Regionalized Plant & Materials List, a sheet on Planting and Maintaining Your Landscape, Zone Maps and Plant Size and Description Guide. These plans will help you achieve professional results, adding value and enjoyment to your property for years to come. Each set of blueprints is a full 18" x 24" in size with clear, complete instructions and easy-to-read type. A sample Landscape Plan is shown below. See Blueprint Price Schedule for ordering information.

CONTEMPORARY LEISURE DECK
Deck ODA021

CAPE COD COTTAGE
Landscape OLA003

REGIONAL ORDER MAP

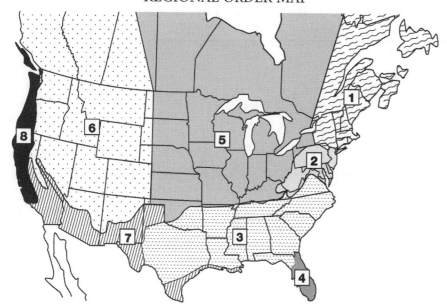

Most Landscape Plans are available with a Plant & Materials List adapted by horticultural experts to 8 different regions of the country. Please specify the Geographic Region when ordering your plan. See Blueprint Price Schedule for ordering information and regional availability.

Region	1	Northeast
Region	2	Mid-Atlantic
Region	3	Deep South
Region	4	Florida & Gulf Coast
Region	5	Midwest
Region	6	Rocky Mountains
Region	7	Southern California & Desert Southwest
Region	8	Northern California & Pacific Northwest

BLUEPRINT PRICE SCHEDULE

Prices guaranteed through December 31, 2003

TIERS	1-SET STUDY PACKAGE	4-SET BUILDING PACKAGE	8-SET BUILDING PACKAGE	1-SET REPRODUCIBLE*
P1	$20	$50	$90	$140
P2	$40	$70	$110	$160
P3	$70	$100	$140	$190
P4	$100	$130	$170	$220
P5	$140	$170	$210	$270
P6	$180	$210	$250	$310
A1	$440	$480	$520	$660
A2	$480	$520	$560	$720
A3	$530	$575	$615	$800
A4	$575	$620	$660	$870
C1	$620	$665	$710	$935
C2	$670	$715	$760	$1000
C3	$715	$760	$805	$1075
C4	$765	$810	$855	$1150
L1	$870	$925	$975	$1300
L2	$945	$1000	$1050	$1420
L3	$1050	$1105	$1155	$1575
L4	$1155	$1210	$1260	$1735
SQ1				.35/SqFt

* Requires a fax number

OPTIONS FOR PLANS IN TIERS A1–L4

Additional Identical Blueprints
in same order for "A1–L4" price plans..$50 per set
Reverse Blueprints (mirror image)
with 4- or 8-set order for "A1–L4" plans...$50 fee per order
Specification Outlines...$10 each
Materials Lists for "A1–C3" plans ....$60 each
Materials Lists for "C4–L4" plans...$70 each

OPTIONS FOR PLANS IN TIERS P1–P6

Additional Identical Blueprints
in same order for "P1–P6" price plans..$10 per set
Reverse Blueprints (mirror image) for "P1–P6" price plans ....$10 fee per order
1 Set of Deck Construction Details ....$14.95 each
Deck Construction Package ....**add $10 to Building Package price**
(includes 1 set of "P1–P6" plans, plus 1 set Standard Deck Construction Details)

IMPORTANT NOTES

- SQ one-set building package includes one set of reproducible vellum construction drawings plus, one set of study blueprints.
- The 1-set study package is marked "not for construction."
- Prices for 4- or 8-set Building Packages honored only at time of original order.
- Some foundations carry a $225 surcharge.
- Right-reading reverse blueprints, if available, will incur a $165 surcharge.
- Additional identical blueprints may be purchased within 60 days of original order.

TO USE THE INDEX, refer to the design number listed in numerical order (a helpful page reference is also given). Note the price tier and refer to the Blueprint Price Schedule above for the cost of one, four or eight sets of blueprints or the cost of a reproducible drawing. Additional prices are shown for identical and reverse blueprint sets, as well as a very useful Materials List for some of the plans. Also note in the Plan Index those plans that have Deck Plans or Landscape Plans. Refer to the schedules above for prices of these plans. The letter "Y" identifies plans that are part of our Quote One® estimating service and those that offer Materials Lists.

TO ORDER, Call toll free 1-800-521-6797 for current pricing and availability prior to mailing the order form. FAX: 1-800-224-6699 or 520-544-3086.

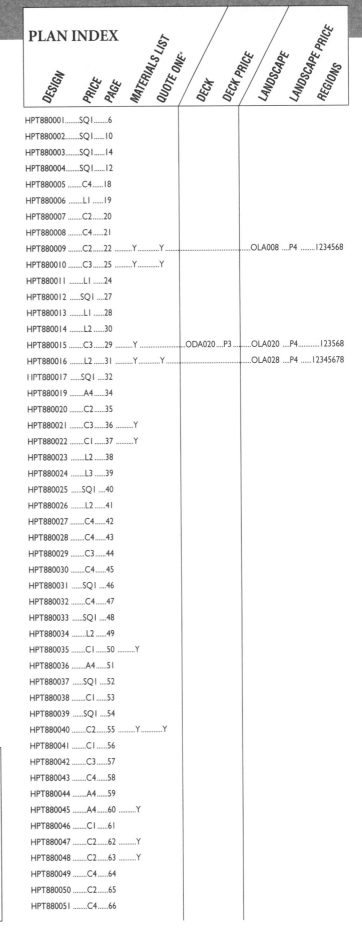

PLAN INDEX

DESIGN	PRICE	PAGE	MATERIALS LIST	QUOTE ONE®	DECK	DECK PRICE	LANDSCAPE	LANDSCAPE PRICE	REGIONS
HPT880001	SQ1	6							
HPT880002	SQ1	10							
HPT880003	SQ1	14							
HPT880004	SQ1	12							
HPT880005	C4	18							
HPT880006	L1	19							
HPT880007	C2	20							
HPT880008	C4	21							
HPT880009	C2	22	Y	Y			OLA008	P4	1234568
HPT880010	C3	25	Y	Y					
HPT880011	L1	24							
HPT880012	SQ1	27							
HPT880013	L1	28							
HPT880014	L2	30							
HPT880015	C3	29	Y		ODA020	P3	OLA020	P4	123568
HPT880016	L2	31	Y	Y			OLA028	P4	12345678
HPT880017	SQ1	32							
HPT880019	A4	34							
HPT880020	C2	35							
HPT880021	C3	36	Y						
HPT880022	C1	37	Y						
HPT880023	L2	38							
HPT880024	L3	39							
HPT880025	SQ1	40							
HPT880026	L2	41							
HPT880027	C4	42							
HPT880028	C4	43							
HPT880029	C3	44							
HPT880030	C4	45							
HPT880031	SQ1	46							
HPT880032	C4	47							
HPT880033	SQ1	48							
HPT880034	L2	49							
HPT880035	C1	50	Y						
HPT880036	A4	51							
HPT880037	SQ1	52							
HPT880038	C1	53							
HPT880039	SQ1	54							
HPT880040	C2	55	Y	Y					
HPT880041	C1	56							
HPT880042	C3	57							
HPT880043	C4	58							
HPT880044	A4	59							
HPT880045	A4	60	Y						
HPT880046	C1	61							
HPT880047	C2	62	Y						
HPT880048	C2	63	Y						
HPT880049	C4	64							
HPT880050	C2	65							
HPT880051	C4	66							

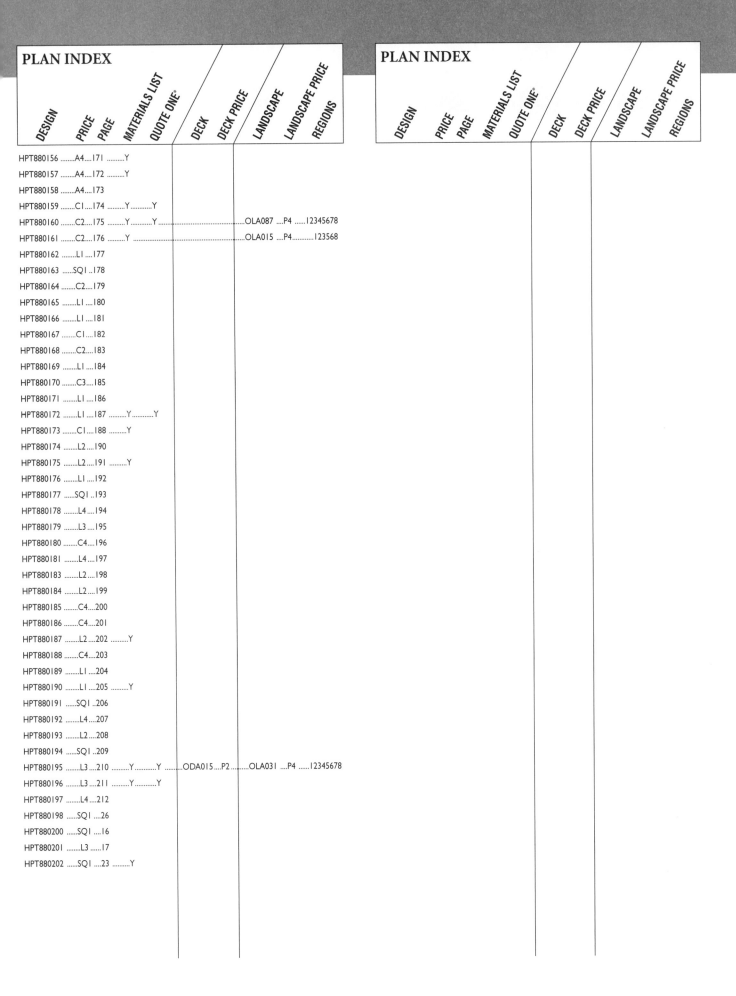

BEFORE FILLING OUT THE ORDER FORM, PLEASE CALL US ON OUR TOLL-FREE BLUEPRINT HOTLINE 1-800-521-6797. YOU MAY WANT TO LEARN MORE ABOUT OUR SERVICES AND PRODUCTS. HERE'S SOME INFORMATION YOU WILL FIND HELPFUL.

OUR EXCHANGE POLICY

With the exception of reproducible plan orders, we will exchange your entire first order for an equal or greater number of blueprints within our plan collection within 90 days of the original order. The entire content of your original order must be returned before an exchange will be processed. Please call our customer service department for your return authorization number and shipping instructions. If the returned blueprints look used, redlined or copied, we will not honor your exchange. Fees for exchanging your blueprints are as follows: 20% of the amount of the original order...plus the difference in cost if exchanging for a design in a higher price bracket or less the difference in cost if exchanging for a design in a lower price bracket. **(Reproducible blueprints are not exchangeable or refundable.)** Please call for current postage and handling prices. Shipping and handling charges are not refundable.

ABOUT REPRODUCIBLES

When purchasing a reproducible you may be required to furnish a fax number. The designer will fax documents that you must sign and return to them before shipping will take place.

ABOUT REVERSE BLUEPRINTS

Although lettering and dimensions will appear backward, reverses will be a useful aid if you decide to flop the plan. See Price Schedule and Plans Index for pricing.

REVISING, MODIFYING AND CUSTOMIZING PLANS

Like many homeowners who buy these plans, you and your builder, architect or engineer may want to make changes to them. We recommend purchase of a reproducible plan for any changes made by your builder, licensed architect or engineer. As set forth below, we cannot assume any responsibility for blueprints which have been changed, whether by you, your builder or by professionals selected by you or referred to you by us, because such individuals are outside our supervision and control.

ARCHITECTURAL AND ENGINEERING SEALS

Some cities and states are now requiring that a licensed architect or engineer review and "seal" a blueprint, or officially approve it, prior to construction due to concerns over energy costs, safety and other factors. Prior to application for a building permit or the start of actual construction, we strongly advise that you consult your local building official who can tell you if such a review is required.

ABOUT THE DESIGNS

The architects and designers whose work appears in this publication are among America's leading residential designers. Each plan was designed to meet the requirements of a nationally recognized model building code in effect at the time and place the plan was drawn. Because national building codes change from time to time, plans may not comply with any such code at the time they are sold to a customer. In addition, building officials may not accept these plans as final construction documents of record as the plans may need to be modified and additional drawings and details added to suit local conditions and requirements. We strongly advise that purchasers consult a licensed architect or engineer, and their local building official, before starting any construction related to these plans.

LOCAL BUILDING CODES AND ZONING REQUIREMENTS

At the time of creation, our plans are drawn to specifications published by the Building Officials and Code Administrators (BOCA) International, Inc.; the Southern Building Code Congress (SBCCI) International, Inc.; the International Conference of Building Officials (ICBO); or the Council of American Building Officials (CABO). Our plans are designed to meet or exceed national building standards. Because of the great differences in geography and climate throughout the United States and Canada, each state, county and municipality has its own building codes, zone requirements, ordinances and building regulations. Your plan may need to be modified to comply with local requirements regarding snow loads, energy codes, soil and seismic conditions and a wide range of other matters. In addition, you may need to obtain permits or inspections from local governments before and in the course of construction. Prior to using blueprints ordered from us, we strongly advise that you consult a licensed architect or engineer—and speak with your local building official— before applying for any permit or beginning construction. We authorize the use of our blueprints on the express condition that you strictly comply with all local building codes, zoning requirements and other applicable laws, regulations, ordinances and requirements. Notice: Plans for homes to be built in Nevada must be re-drawn by a Nevada-registered professional. Consult your building official for more information on this subject.

TOLL FREE
1-800-521-6797

REGULAR OFFICE HOURS:
8:00 a.m.-9:00 p.m. EST, Monday-Friday

If we receive your order by 3:00 p.m. EST, Monday-Friday, we'll process it and ship within **two business days**. When ordering by phone, please have your credit card or check information ready. We'll also ask you for the Order Form Key Number at the bottom of the order form.

By FAX: Copy the Order Form on the next page and send it on our FAX line: 1-800-224-6699 or 520-544-3086.

Canadian Customers
Order Toll Free 1-877-223-6389

HOME PLANNERS, LLC wholly owned by Hanley-Wood, LLC
3275 WEST INA ROAD, SUITE 110 • TUCSON, ARIZONA • 85741

DISCLAIMER

The designers we work with have put substantial care and effort into the creation of their blueprints. However, because they cannot provide on-site consultation, supervision and control over actual construction, and because of the great variance in local building requirements, building practices and soil, seismic, weather and other conditions, WE CANNOT MAKE ANY WARRANTY, EXPRESS OR IMPLIED, WITH RESPECT TO THE CONTENT OR USE OF THE BLUEPRINTS, INCLUDING BUT NOT LIMITED TO ANY WARRANTY OF MERCHANTABILITY OR OF FITNESS FOR A PARTICULAR PURPOSE. **ITEMS, PRICES, TERMS AND CONDITIONS ARE SUBJECT TO CHANGE WITHOUT NOTICE. REPRODUCIBLE PLAN ORDERS MAY REQUIRE A CUSTOMER'S SIGNED RELEASE BEFORE SHIPPING.**

TERMS AND CONDITIONS

These designs are protected under the terms of United States Copyright Law and may not be copied or reproduced in any way, by any means, unless you have purchased Reproducibles which clearly indicate your right to copy or reproduce. We authorize the use of your chosen design as an aid in the construction of one single family home only. You may not use this design to build a second or multiple dwellings without purchasing another blueprint or blueprints or paying additional design fees.

HOW MANY BLUEPRINTS DO YOU NEED?

Although a standard building package may satisfy many states, cities and counties, some plans may require certain changes. For your convenience, we have developed a Reproducible plan which allows a local professional to modify and make up to 10 copies of your revised plan. As our plans are all copyright protected, with your purchase of the Reproducible, we will supply you with a Copyright release letter. The number of copies you may need: 1 for owner; 3 for builder; 2 for local building department and 1-3 sets for your mortgage lender.

ORDER TOLL FREE!

For information about any of our services or to order call
1-800-521-6797

Browse our website:
www.eplans.com

BLUEPRINTS ARE NOT REFUNDABLE EXCHANGES ONLY

For Customer Service, call toll free
1-888-690-1116.

THE BASIC BLUEPRINT PACKAGE

Rush me the following (please refer to the Plans Index and Price Schedule in this section):

___ Set(s) of reproducibles*, plan number(s) _____ $_____
    indicate foundation type _____ surcharge (if applicable): $_____
___ Set(s) of blueprints, plan number(s) _____ $_____
    indicate foundation type _____ surcharge (if applicable): $_____
___ Additional identical blueprints (standard or reverse) in same order @ $50 per set $_____
___ Reverse blueprints @ $50 fee per order. Right-reading reverse @ $165 surcharge $_____

IMPORTANT EXTRAS

Rush me the following:

___ Materials List: $60 (Must be purchased with Blueprint set.) Add $10 for Schedule C4–L4 plans $_____
___ **Quote One®** Summary Cost Report @ $29.95 for one, $14.95 for each additional,
    for plans _____ $_____
    Building location: City _____ Zip Code _____
___ **Quote One®** Material Cost Report @ $120 Schedules P1–C3; $130 Schedules C4–L4,
    for plan _____ (Must be purchased with Blueprints set.) $_____
    Building location: City _____ Zip Code _____
___ Specification Outlines @ $10 each $_____
___ Detail Sets @ $14.95 each; any two $22.95; any three $29.95; all four for $39.95 (save $19.85) $_____
    ❑ Plumbing ❑ Electrical ❑ Construction ❑ Mechanical
___ Home Furniture Planner @ $15.95 each $_____

DECK BLUEPRINTS

(Please refer to the Plans Index and Price Schedule in this section)

___ Set(s) of Deck Plan _____ $_____
___ Additional identical blueprints in same order @ $10 per set. $_____
___ Reverse blueprints @ $10 fee per order. $_____
___ Set of Standard Deck Details @ $14.95 per set. $_____
___ Set of Complete Deck Construction Package (Best Buy!) Add $10 to Building Package.
    Includes Custom Deck Plan _____ Plus Standard Deck Details

LANDSCAPE BLUEPRINTS

(Please refer to the Plans Index and Price Schedule in this section.)

___ Set(s) of Landscape Plan _____ $_____
___ Additional identical blueprints in same order @ $10 per set $_____
___ Reverse blueprints @ $10 fee per order $_____

Please indicate appropriate region of the country for Plant & Material List. Region _____

POSTAGE AND HANDLING *SIGNATURE IS REQUIRED FOR ALL DELIVERIES.*	1–3 sets	4+ sets
DELIVERY No CODs (Requires street address—No P.O. Boxes) •Regular Service (Allow 7–10 business days delivery) •Priority (Allow 4–5 business days delivery) •Express (Allow 3 business days delivery)	 ❑ $20.00 ❑ $25.00 ❑ $35.00	 ❑ $25.00 ❑ $35.00 ❑ $45.00
OVERSEAS DELIVERY	fax, phone or mail for quote	

Note: All delivery times are from date Blueprint Package is shipped.

POSTAGE (From box above) $_____
SUBTOTAL $_____
SALES TAX (AZ & MI residents, please add appropriate state and local sales tax.) $_____
TOTAL (Subtotal and tax) $_____

YOUR ADDRESS (please print legibly)

Name _____

Street _____

City _____ State _____ Zip _____

Daytime telephone number (required) (_____) _____

* Fax number (required for reproducible orders) _____
TeleCheck® Checks By Phone℠ available

FOR CREDIT CARD ORDERS ONLY

Credit card number _____ Exp. Date: (M/Y) _____

Check one ❑ Visa ❑ MasterCard ❑ Discover Card ❑ American Express

Order Form Key

Signature (required) _____ | HPT88 |

Please check appropriate box: ❑ Licensed Builder-Contractor ❑ Homeowner

ORDER TOLL FREE!
1-800-521-6797

BY FAX: Copy the order form above and send it on our FAXLINE: 1-800-224-6699 OR 520-544-3086

1 BIGGEST & BEST

1001 of our best-selling plans in one volume. 1,074 to 7,275 square feet. 704 pgs $12.95 1K1

2 ONE-STORY

450 designs for all lifestyles. 800 to 4,900 square feet. 384 pgs $9.95 OS

3 MORE ONE-STORY

475 superb one-level plans from 800 to 5,000 square feet. 448 pgs $9.95 MO2

4 TWO-STORY

443 designs for one-and-a-half and two stories. 1,500 to 6,000 square feet. 448 pgs $9.95 TS

5 VACATION

430 designs for recreation, retirement and leisure. 448 pgs $9.95 VS3

6 HILLSIDE

208 designs for split-levels, bi-levels, multi-levels and walkouts. 224 pgs $9.95 HH

7 FARMHOUSE

300 Fresh Designs from Classic to Modern. 320 pgs. $10.95 FCP

8 COUNTRY HOUSES

208 unique home plans that combine traditional style and modern livability. 224 pgs $9.95 CN

9 BUDGET-SMART

200 efficient plans from 7 top designers, that you can really afford to build! 224 pgs $8.95 BS

10 BARRIER-FREE

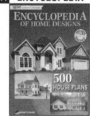

Over 1,700 products and 51 plans for accessible living. 128 pgs $15.95 UH

11 ENCYCLOPEDIA

500 exceptional plans for all styles and budgets—the best book of its kind! 528 pgs $9.95 ENC

12 ENCYCLOPEDIA II

500 completely new plans. Spacious and stylish designs for every budget and taste. 352 pgs $9.95 E2

13 AFFORDABLE

300 Modest plans for savvy homebuyers.256 pgs. $9.95 AH2

14 VICTORIAN

210 striking Victorian and Farmhouse designs from today's top designers. 224 pgs $15.95 VDH2

15 ESTATE

Dream big! Eighteen designers showcase their biggest and best plans. 224 pgs $16.95 EDH3

16 LUXURY

170 lavish designs, over 50% brand-new plans added to a most elegant collection. 192 pgs $12.95 LD3

17 EUROPEAN STYLES

200 homes with a unique flair of the Old World. 224 pgs $15.95 EURO

18 COUNTRY CLASSICS

Donald Gardner's 101 best Country and Traditional home plans. 192 pgs $17.95 DAG

19 COUNTRY

85 Charming Designs from American Home Gallery. 160 pgs. $17.95 CTY

20 TRADITIONAL

85 timeless designs from the Design Traditions Library. 160 pgs $17.95 TRA

21 COTTAGES

245 Delightful retreats from 825 to 3,500 square feet. 256 pgs. $10.95 COOL

22 CABINS TO VILLAS

Enchanting Homes for Mountain Sea or Sun, from the Sater collection. 144 pgs $19.95 CCV

23 CONTEMPORARY

The most complete and imaginative collection of contemporary designs available anywhere. 256 pgs. $10.95 CM2

24 FRENCH COUNTRY

Live every day in the French countryside using these plans, landscapes and interiors. 192 pgs. $14.95 PN

25 SOUTHERN

207 homes rich in Southern styling and comfort. 240 pgs $8.95 SH

26 SOUTHWESTERN

138 designs that capture the spirit of the Southwest. 144 pgs $10.95 SW

27 SHINGLE-STYLE

155 Home plans from Classic Colonials to Breezy Bungalows. 192 pgs. $12.95 SNG

28 NEIGHBORHOOD

170 designs with the feel of main street America. 192 pgs $12.95 TND

29 CRAFTSMAN

170 Home plans in the Craftsman and Bungalow style. 192 pgs $12.95 CC

30 GRAND VISTAS

200 Homes with a View. 224 pgs. $10.95 GV

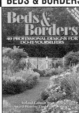
Book Order Form

To order your books, just check the box of the book numbered below and complete the coupon. We will process your order and ship it from our office within two business days. Send coupon and check (in U.S. funds).

YES! Please send me the books I've indicated:

1:1K1 ....$12.95	17:EURO...$15.95	33:NA..........$8.95
2:OS $9.95	18:DAG $17.95	34:NOS $14.95
3:MO2 ....$9.95	19:CTY $17.95	35:SOD $19.95
4:TS $9.95	20:TRA $17.95	36:NL2 ......$9.95
5:VS3 ....$9.95	21:COOL ...$10.95	37:SM2 ......$8.95
6:HH $9.95	22:CCV $19.95	38:GLP $19.95
7:FCP $10.95	23:CM2 ....$10.95	39:ECL $14.95
8:CN $9.95	24:PN $14.95	40:BYL $14.95
9:BS $8.95	25:SH $8.95	41:BB $14.95
10:UH $15.95	26:SW $10.95	42:LPBG ...$19.95
11:ENC.......$9.95	27:SNG $12.95	43:YG2 ......$9.95
12:E2 ....$9.95	28:TND $12.95	44:GG2 ......$9.95
13:AH2 ....$9.95	29:CC $12.95	45:DP2 ......$9.95
14:VDH2 ...$15.95	30:GV $10.95	46:HBP $14.95
15:EDH3 ...$16.95	31:MFH $17.95	47:BYC.....$14.95
16:LD3 ....$12.95	32:WF $10.95	48:BYV.....$14.95

Books Subtotal $_____
ADD Postage and Handling (allow 4–6 weeks for delivery) $__4.00__
Sales Tax: (AZ & MI residents, add state and local sales tax.) $_____
YOUR TOTAL (Subtotal, Postage/Handling, Tax) $_____

YOUR ADDRESS (PLEASE PRINT)

Name _____
Street _____
City _____ State _____ Zip _____
Phone (_____) _____ — _____

YOUR PAYMENT

TeleCheck® Checks By Phone℠ available
Check one: ❑ Check ❑ Visa ❑ MasterCard ❑ Discover ❑ American Express
Required credit card information:

Credit Card Number _____
Expiration Date (Month/Year)_____ / _____
Signature Required _____

Home Planners, LLC
3275 W. Ina Road, Suite 110, Dept. BK, Tucson, AZ 85741

HPT88

Canadian Customers Order Toll Free 1-877-223-6389

HEAT-N-GLO
1-888-427-3973
WWW.HEATNGLO.COM

Heat-N-Glo offers quality gas, woodburning and electric fireplaces, including gas log sets, stoves, and inserts for preexisting fireplaces. Now available gas grills and outdoor fireplaces. Send for a free brochure.

Ideas for your next project. Beautiful, durable, elegant low-maintenance millwork, mouldings, balustrade systems and much more. For your free catalog please call us at 1-800-446-3040 or visit www.stylesolutionsinc.com.

ARISTOKRAFT
ONE MASTERBRAND CABINETS DRIVE
JASPER, IN 47546
(812) 482-2527
WWW.ARISTOKRAFT.COM

Aristokraft offers you superb value, outstanding quality and great style that fit your budget. Transform your great ideas into reality with popular styles and features that reflect your taste and lifestyle. $5.00

THERMA-TRU DOORS
1687 WOODLANDS DRIVE
MAUMEE, OH 43537
1-800-THERMA-TRU
WWW.THERMATRU.COM

The undisputed brand leader, Therma-Tru specializes in fiberglass and steel entry doors for every budget. Excellent craftsmanship, energy efficiency and variety make Therma-Tru the perfect choice for all your entry door needs.

225 GARDEN, LANDSCAPE
AND PROJECT PLANS
TO ORDER, CALL
1-800-322-6797

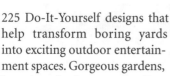

225 Do-It-Yourself designs that help transform boring yards into exciting outdoor entertainment spaces. Gorgeous gardens, luxurious landscapes, dazzling decks and other outdoor amenities. Complete construction blueprints available for every project. Only $19.95 (plus $4 shipping/handling).

HAVE WE GOT PLANS FOR YOU!

Your online source for home designs and ideas. Find thousands of plans from the nation's top designers...all in one place. Plus, links to the best known names in building supplies and services.